IRRESISTIBLE LEADERSHIP

*Ideas & Tools from Top Trainers, Speakers &
Consultants to Help You Be a Leader
Others Want to Follow — Both at Work & at Home*

Compiled by Doug Smart

IRRESISTIBLE LEADERSHIP

Managing Editor: Gayle Smart
Editor: Gelia Dolcimascolo
Assistant Editor: Sara Kahan
Book Designer: Paula Chance
Copyright ©1999

Disclaimer: This book is a compilation of ideas
from numerous experts who have each contributed a chapter.
As such, the views expressed in each chapter are those of the authors
and not necessarily the views of James & Brookfield Publishers.

For more information, contact:
James & Brookfield Publishers
P.O. Box 768024
Roswell, GA 30076
℗ 770-587-9784

Library of Congress Catalog Number 99-071846

ISBN: 0-9658893-9-4

10 9 8 7 6 5 4 3 2 1

This book is dedicated to everyone who has ever said,
"Follow me."

The lectures you deliver may be wise and true,

But I'd rather get my lessons by observing what you do.

I may not understand the high advice you like to give,

But there's no misunderstanding how you act and how you live.

— Edgar A. Guest

CONTENTS

COMMUNICATION TOOLS FOR TOMORROW'S LEADERS

By Mary Kay Kurzweg

Are you ready? Are you ready to lead, motivate and manage tomorrow's work force?

It is becoming increasingly difficult just to maintain your position while organizations determined to increase their growth rate must constantly search for new ideas, systems and strategies. You cannot just survive; you need to learn to thrive in today's rapidly changing business climate. We are looking at a business world that continues to move faster, grow more complex and require finely honed skills.

The individuals and companies that fail to keep up in the twenty-first century will spiral down, becoming smaller, less profitable and probably extinct. Those organizations and individuals, however, who do anticipate and then meet or exceed the ever-changing customer needs will know success and great satisfaction.

A major factor in the success of organizations in the past has been effective communication. In the future, it will be crucial. Only through efficient, focused communication can we stay ahead of and respond pro-actively to changing customer expectations or preferences.

The men and women in leadership positions must have tremendous communication skills to stimulate the back-and-forth flow of ideas, to express a vision of the future that excites others and to help mesh every individual's particular goals and aspirations with the organization's "big picture" plans. Of all the traits that lead to business and personal success, communication is probably the most important. An idea is useless unless others can understand it. Without communication, a team will not move toward a common goal. Successful interaction with customers, suppliers and coworkers plays a vital role in the growth of the business.

Great communicators can achieve great heights. Former President Ronald Reagan, media star Oprah Winfrey and movie mogul Steven Spielberg owe a large part of their successes to their ability to connect with huge, diverse audiences. Almost all of us have come into contact with great communicators — those people who had the ability to express ideas and entice others to act. Who have been three "great communicators" in your life?

Were these people, the famous and the not-so-famous, born with gifts the rest of us do not have? Have they simply been blessed with an amazing ability to speak and write great ideas, to entertain, or to tap into the emotions that make us want to follow their lead? Of course not. What they have done is master the communication fundamentals, the framework that has allowed their messages and, hence, themselves to soar.

We can all improve our communication skills. As a professional speaker, I have spent thousands of hours studying how people communicate. I have given particular attention to those speakers and writers in our society who have reached the pinnacle of their profession. The fundamental guidelines that all great communicators share, and that every twenty-first century leader must use, can be implemented by all of us.

Before You Begin

Any type of communication, whether it's a formal speech to several hundred people or an informal telephone call to a business colleague, must be focused on two critical questions:

1. What do you (the speaker/writer) want to accomplish?

2. Who is your audience, and what are their particular characteristics, needs and wants?

What you want to happen during communication can be a multitude of things. You may want to simply relay some information. Or you may need to ask the other person for something, such as a favor or to place an order. When comedian Jerry Sienfeld does his stand-up comedy act at a club, he has one goal: to entertain the audience. When noted author and motivational speaker Zig Ziglar speaks before a group of entrepreneurs, his primary goal is to pass on specific business building tips while also offering words of inspiration.

Whatever it is you want to accomplish must be known beforehand to make your statements clear, focused and easy for the reader or listener to grasp. Ask yourself the following questions as you begin to prepare a speech, presentation or written communication:

- What do I want my audience to know?
- What reaction do I want to stimulate in my audience?
- What do I want to accomplish through my communication?
- What, if anything, do I want my audience to do with what I've communicated?

Once you know what you want to achieve, you must focus on your audience to tailor your message to meet their needs and expectations. Who is the audience? What are they like? What are their expectations, goals, ways of communicating?

Knowing your audience is critical. Stephen King's readers don't buy one of his novels to spend a quiet evening gaining business insights; they buy his books to be entertained, even frightened. Teenagers don't attend a Beastie Boys concert to hear Bach; they want to hear hard rock.

Before speaking or writing, answer these questions:

- Who is the audience? (One person? A group? An auditorium filled with people?)
- What are they expecting from me?
- What possible resistance or reluctance might I encounter regarding what I have said or written?
- Why should the audience care?

This last sentence is critical. You must connect what you are communicating with a need or interest of your audience. Again using Oprah Winfrey as an example, her talk show is the most successful in the history of television. Her audience has come to expect Oprah to do certain things, interview a particular group of people. If she deviates from the audience's expectations — such as using the show to promote time-share condominiums in Florida — she would be in real danger of alienating and ultimately losing her audience. To make your communication stand out and become more effective, have a clear understanding at the beginning of what you want to achieve and what your audience expects.

Planning

Once you know and understand what you want to accomplish and what your audience expects, you must plan how you will deliver your message. This preparation is a critical phase to successful communication. We are all overwhelmed with information and often face time challenges, limiting our ability to really listen.

Determine what style of presentation is most appropriate for you to meet your objectives. Listed are the three main styles of presentation and the situations when each is most appropriate to use.

READING — Appropriate when legal issues are involved; when making statements to the media that will be quoted and must, therefore, be precise; and if preparation time is minimal.

MEMORIZING — Use for short presentations only. It can be impressive, but sometimes sounds mechanical or programmed. Additionally, it limits your opportunity for spontaneity.

IMPROMPTU/REHEARSED — This is often used for informal but professional situations, such as while attending a meeting or making a small presentation to a group. Oftentimes, the speaker will have note cards that contain key ideas, should he or she need them.

Note that each of the above methods requires preparation and practice, even the impromptu presentation. American humorist Mark Twain said, "It usually takes no more than three weeks to prepare a good impromptu speech." He was right!

Once you have determined what method you are going to use, you must decide how to present the information. In public speaking circles, there's a saying that would seem cliché if it were not so true:

Tell your audience what you're going to say.

Say it.

Tell your audience what you said.

To put it another way, each of your communications should have an introduction (beginning), a body (middle), and a wrap-up (end). This is true if you are writing a memo, making a presentation in front of the board of directors or addressing a crowd.

Here's an example. My notes are in brackets:

Dear Paul:

[Introduction] Our HR Department has finished updating our Employee Orientation handbook. [Body: What you want the reader to do] We will contract out for the printing, and I would like your company to submit a bid. I need your quote by the 10th of next month. [Wrap-up] Please contact me to discuss specifics, such as size, number of pages, etc. Thanks.

The author has clearly stated his reason for writing and has spelled out exactly what he needs from the reader and when he needs it.

Also, be aware of any potential time constraints that may be in the way of delivering your message. While working for the Daily Point of Light Award, a project aimed at making volunteerism more visible in our country, I often attended functions at the White House. At a reception in the Rose Garden honoring a large group of volunteers, the honorees were told they could each speak with President Bush for approximately one to two minutes. One woman, obviously excited to meet the President and proud of her accomplishments, went into great detail about her program and began to run well past her allotted time. President Bush listened politely, although the White House organizers were clearly getting nervous as the woman gushed on. One White House staff member finally had to cut the woman off.

The point is that the woman did not take into account the time allotment she was given at the beginning. Whatever message she may have been able to offer the President was probably lost as she rambled on. A few well-thought-out sentences would have been more effective.

Think in terms of a beginning, middle and end, and understand the constraints that may block or hinder your message.

Speeches and Presentations

Every successful speech or presentation accomplishes each of the following:

- Gets the audience's attention
- Has meaning and value for the audience
- Creates cause for action
- Is memorable

Getting the audience's attention simply means that we must quickly engage the listener. Psychologists say we have only 30 seconds to capture an audience. Given the limited attention span of the average person, you must begin quickly and be compelling enough to stimulate interest in listening. Author and speaker George Jessel makes this point in a humorous way when he says, "If you haven't struck oil in your first three minutes, stop boring."

Being of value for the audience requires that you know your topic and know as much as possible about your audience; what they want and expect. This includes the number of people who will attend as well as their gender, age, educational level, occupations and their knowledge of your topic. You will also have to discern how much you will have to do to prove yourself to the group.

To create cause for action reminds us that most communication is done to compel others to support you or your position. The most effective communicators and leaders are those who move others to act. Influence, not authority, is the key to success for the twenty-first century leader.

Be memorable, and your message will last. This may be done by a snappy ending, the introduction of unique visual aids or other means. The important thing is to make your message stand out from the crowd.

Never forget the importance of body language and eye contact. The best written speech when poorly delivered is powerless. Keep your body language aligned with what you are saying. A speaker who delivers a painful message with a big smile on his face loses his credibility. When a leader claims to be enthusiastic about a new project and does not look excited, she will not be believed. If leaders are not believable, they are not followed.

Word Choices

Once you acknowledge what you want to accomplish, you must attempt to create as vivid a picture as possible in the reader or listener's mind to help them understand. You do this through the words you use. The following are tips and suggestions to use the best word choices possible:

- Use Specific Words

Use specific, rather than abstract, words to make your message more interesting. Abstract words are less precise, and therefore make it more difficult for the reader or listener to create a visual mental picture about your topic. Abstract words are those like fruit, hot, cold, tree, flower, and so on. Specific words are more exact, such as apple, ninety degrees, minus thirteen degrees Celsius, oak tree, and daisy.

A great example of using specific as opposed to abstract words is shown in the following excerpt from the Stephen King novel, *Misery*:

As [Paul] was rolling across the parlor, the scrapbook under the coffee table caught his eye again. MEMORY LANE. It was as big as a folio Shakespeare play and as thick as a family Bible.

Notice the precise words: parlor, scrapbook, coffee table, family bible. Do you have a clear image in your mind about what is happening and where it is taking place? Would the above three sentences have been as visually stimulating if King had written, "As [Paul] was rolling across the room, the big book under the table caught his eye again."? Of course not. Always use specific words to help the reader (or listener) create a vividly clear mental picture.

- Use Action Verbs

Action verbs add punch and texture as well as excitement to communications. Avoid forms of the verbs "to have" and "to be," which are passive and thus uninteresting.

Notice the difference in these two sentences:

It was hot outside. (passive)

The temperature outside hovered near ninety degrees. (active)

Which of these two sentences evokes a stronger, clearer image?

Notice the use of action verbs in the following passage from Wallace Stegner's novel, *Angle of Repose*, for which he won a Pulitzer Prize:

They undressed in the dark, kissed lightly, and lay down. The wind blew through the cabin, bellying the curtains bunched on their wire, waking a curl of flame in the fire. Out the open door the hillside swam in pale light, and in the visible strip of sky a cloud . . . blazed like something out of a smelter pot.

The verbs *undressed, kissed, blew, bellying, bunched,* and so on give movement and action to the description. They engage the reader and make the writing strong, forceful and confident. The same can be done with any type of communication, such as with this segment of a business letter:

It was nice meeting you yesterday. Our conversation was very helpful, and we at XYZ have high hopes of helping you. (passive)

versus:

Thank you for meeting with me yesterday. I enjoyed our conversation, and we at XYZ look forward to assisting your future efforts. (active)

Although the two examples seem similar, there is a subtle difference in good writing and weaker writing. Make your verbs stronger and more active, and your communication will become more forceful and confident.

Appeal to All Five Senses

A common mistake is to describe a thing or situation only by how it looks. However, sight is only one of our five senses. Using more than one sense will make your descriptions more vivid and more memorable.

The following is a brief passage from Eudora Welty's book, *The Optimist's Daughter,* which won her a Pulitzer Prize and happens to take place in my hometown, New Orleans. The following excerpt is an excellent example of an author appealing to more than one sense:

The interior of the cab reeked of bourbon, and as they passed under a streetlight she saw a string of cheap green beads on the floor. When she let down the glass window for air, she heard the mocking trumpet playing with a band from some distance away.

This is a great description. Can you smell the cab, see the beads, feel the air on her face, hear the trumpet? In one short paragraph, Welty hit on four of the five senses.

Study and hone your word choices to make your communication more effective and more interesting.

Polishing

Once you prepare the material you want to deliver or present, you must practice and hone the message to make it as simple and as clear as possible. I call this final stage polishing. To do this, consider the following:

• Read out loud. Note the places (words or phrases) that might not be as clear as you would like. These are often the places that need to be simplified or changed. A simple message will stand out from more complicated messages because your audience will be more comfortable and attentive when your message is listener friendly.

• Practice, practice, practice. (For written projects, this would be revise, revise, revise.) This builds confidence and fluency. Isak Dinesen, author of the book, *Out of Africa*, said that she wrote a little every day, without hope and without despair. Your communication will improve as you revise/practice.

• Enlist others to help. For a speech or presentation, make a practice run in front of one or two or a small group of friends. Ask for their feedback as to which sections went well and those places that were confusing or seemed to lag in energy. For written projects, have one or more associates read a draft. A fresh set of eyes will almost always catch something that you overlooked.

Bringing it All Together

Speaking and communicating with others, especially large groups, can be scary stuff. Many of my clients ask me if they will ever get over the fear of public speaking. I have to admit that some do, but most learn to control the fear. They learn to channel the fear into enthusiasm and excitement. You can do the same.

Some PHYSICAL stress reducers include:

• Deep breathing. A few deep breaths before you begin.

• Isometric exercises. Tense and then relax your shoulders, arms, legs, etc.

• Relaxation techniques, such as meditation. Spend a few quiet minutes remembering you are there to deliver an important message. Don't let your ego get in the way of the message.

• Vigorous exercises. I like to take brisk walks.

Some PSYCHOLOGICAL stress reducers are:

• Maintain a positive attitude. Think of the best/worst scenario, then laugh at the worst and go for the best.

• Over-prepare. Channel your nervousness into preparation. Like an Olympian, know that you are ready for your event. Go for the Gold!

• Anticipate possible challenges or problems. Be prepared for the negative and make it a positive part of the presentation. Ronald Reagan had us all laughing when he was running for reelection and some questioned his age. His reply was that he refused to allow the youth and inexperience of his opponent to become an issue.

Answering Questions

Try to be as succinct and as clear as possible.

When you don't know an answer, admit it, and say you will find out and get back to the person.

Value the hostile question. At least the person is passionate enough about the subject to get upset. Reply in a calm way.

Guide the off-the-subject question back and tactfully bring the long-winded comment to a conclusion.

End the limited-interest question by suggesting that the participant see you afterward to discuss one on one.

In some cases the audience may be too shy to ask questions. In this case, try to say the following:

"I am often asked . . ."

"Someone once asked me . . ."

"Suppose someone asked? . . ."

Speaking, writing and communicating effectively will make a huge difference in your life and your leadership abilities. These are skills that can be learned. The ideas and suggestions that I have provided should go a long way toward making you a better communicator and therefore a more effective leader. The great leaders of tomorrow — those men and women thriving in the twenty-first century — will be the people who help others to grow, prosper and be their best.

T.S. Elliot told of people who dreamed of creating systems so perfect that no one will need to be good. We know this concept is a fantasy. Communication skills, no matter how finely structured, cannot be substituted for authenticity, love and understanding. With the proper skills, we can express these qualities far more effectively. The expression of these core qualities nourishes and reinforces the characteristics in us and in those with whom we live and work. As we communicate more effectively, we grow and allow others to grow as well.

ABOUT
MARY KAY KURZWEG

*I*f *communication is an art, Mary Kay should be listed as a rare find. With a background in education, business and the volunteer sector, she shares her wealth of experience and practical knowledge with audiences worldwide. Besides serving as President of MKK & Co., she is an award-winning speaker and writer. Her focus is on showing individuals that they make a difference and providing tools for transformation to a more confident and calm being. In a light-hearted manner, Mary Kay explains the factors that influence self-assurance and tells how to capitalize on these factors to become more effective leaders, powerful participants and dynamic speakers. She speaks on the subjects of change, business etiquette, presentation skills, stress management and peak performance. Her diverse client list includes: Edison Electric Institute, Landmark Incentive Marketing (Bangkok), National Institutes of Health, Professional Secretaries International, Social Security Administration, White Mountain Apache Reservation and the Young Presidents Organization.*

Contact information:
MKK & Co.
215 Stella Street
Metairie, LA 70005
✆ (800) 493-2983
✆ (504) 833-0277
fax (504) 835-7733
e-mail: MKKurzweg@aol.com
web: www.callmarykay.com

DEVELOP LEADERSHIP
FROM WITHIN

by D.J. Harrington

We must develop our internal customer in the hopes of servicing our external customers. I know from years of sales and leadership experience with General Motors, Mohawk Carpet and Marietta Drapery that unless we nurture and mold our internal customers — whether they are our immediate departmental colleagues or the lonely shipping clerk — our external customers will be gravely underserviced. By the end of this chapter you should understand the importance of treating the customer right — before, during and after the delivery of your product or service — and you will appreciate the role leadership plays in it.

Most phone calls we receive in our Phone Logic office in Atlanta, Georgia are from the directors of businesses. They engage our service to help with their C.S.I., or Customer Service Index. In response I ask a series of questions, such as: How often does your parts and service department meet to work on deficiencies or address problems with your C.S.I.? The answer is always the same: They do not meet, or they meet maybe once a year. No wonder they seek outside help. They do admit to having "get it off your chest" meetings so people air their gripes, but nobody takes notes. Instead they eat their pizzas and go home. Everyone feels better and does better, right? Not! The next time a complaint comes up, it's the same routine. Everyone sounds off, and nothing gets changed. No mistakes are curtailed or corrected.

A company should plan monthly meetings with specifc agendas and constructive information that is disseminated to all team members. This way everyone receives the same message at the same time, and no one can claim not having prior knowledge of future pertinent changes. All questions are answered collectively, and everyone has a chance to provide input. This is a perfect time to train your people and use lessons of leadership to improve people skills.

The late Cavett Robert, founder of the National Speakers Association, reminded speakers and trainers that he did not care what kind of business a person had. His message at the national convention applied to every company: "We are all in the people business . . . knowing not just what they want to buy . . . but why they buy it."

I want to hear my clients say words like, "I'm with you, DJ. You have integrity and good customer standards, you believe in God and the customer — and you're good to your people." They follow me because of who I am. Price or product does not affect my sales as much as I do. Customers read people quickly, and they buy you and your personal image first, your company second, and buy your product or service third. If people buy in that order, should we sell to them in that order? The answer is yes!

We need to develop our internal customers so that we can grow together. America is full of business people who lead from a distance and present a coveted image to the employees with an airy attitude that they are the boss. Everyone else is just an employee. That egostical thinking is prevalent not only throughout the United States, it also flourishes in Europe, Australia and Canada. If a leader wants to develop his people, he or she concentrates on their hearts first and then asks them for their hands.

I was a successful sales manager for a European company called Berensohn, AG — a company located in Hamburg, West Germany. Before I worked for them, they came to the United States and ran ads in the *Wall Street Journal* for savvy, professional men and women to represent their premium gift line. While working a temporary job my wife,

Sheila, met a lady named Donna whose husband, Ed Martasin worked for Berensohn. Donna deduced that her husband would probably have to hire a salesperson to replace a new hire on his team because the typist who transcribed it had omitted the new hire's actual level of performance from the impressive resumé. Purely typographical? No, typical. To what level of performance is a serious applicant willing to go to qualify for a desirable job? A resumé is usually a short-cut way of providing information that only surfaces once an applicant rolls up his sleeves and begins working. Ed Martasin, was then a Director of Southern Region for Berensohn. I arrived at Ed's home at precisely the time when my wife had set the appointment to interview for the job of sales trainer. I made it through the preliminary interview. Little did I know that job was going to be a great opportunity for me.

The interviewing continued for a second day at the Holiday Inn in downtown Atlanta. The initial interview separated the good applicants from the undesirable ones. The masses had applied for a handful of jobs. An important man from Germany was telling every applicant — so-called "sales trainers" — that we needed to take the "sample" bag filled with everything from pens and letter openers to fine, replicated gold ingots that were actually cigarette lighters. We had to use these products to prove that we were good enough to represent the company. Every single item on their product list was a premium gift at an expensive price. The clientele which would be interested in Berensohn's line included board of director members or presidents of Fortune 500 companies. These clients make important decisions quickly. The gifts I sold would land in the laps of the 10% accounts, known as the "A" accounts. Each sales person made a good share of the profit by selling to such companies. Most of the sales people who were applying for the Berensohn jobs refused to take the sample bag and "cold-call" the streets. They felt they already had ample experience; at least their resumes said they did. They could not see that during this exercise they could have been paving the road to their own success. For them the road to success was started, but fear of failure stopped the road's construction. We were instructed by the company director, Max Herman, from Hamburg, "You need to lead by example and judge by results to be considered for the job." He then told the group to sell from the sample bag for the next two days and return to the Holiday Inn with sales orders in hand.

Only about 20% of the applicants returned. Most of the sample cases were actually brought back by spouses or family members — and not by the qualified applicant. Since I had made the most sales, I was hired on the spot for the Southeastern United States as field sales trainer "to sell door-to-door until there is no more." Here in America the sales trainer's position is quite frequently held by someone who has not been completely successful in actual sales. The German companies, however, want someone training their sales team who has experience and has broken sales records . . . someone who will lead by example.

As soon as I was hired, I worked with each sales person one-on-one in the field. We ate breakfast, lunch and dinner together. I traveled to the next representative and repeated my schedule of selling Monday through Friday. My travels spanned the entire Southeastern United States, section by section. I broke sales records unsurpassed by any other new sales team, and this prompted my boss to send Max, a consultant, to accompany me. Max heard things such as, "DJ cares for me and my family, and when he askes me to go that extra mile, well, I do." Seek their hearts, and then ask for their hands.

Leaders develop the internal customer first and do not have to worry about cultivating the external customer because it happens naturally if the internal customer develops first. I told one group recently, "If I were teaching athletics today, and you were a student learning to be a pole-vaulter, I would tell you to put your heart over the bar first, and the rest of your body will follow." Such is true with leadership.

My tips are not amazing brainstorms but common sense that you can pass along to others throughout your career. Most importantly, you have to sell yourself and your organization 100% before selling your product or service. You must sell in that order, because people buy in that order. If you do, you have learned the science of selling. Selling is a science of persuasiveness, or assuring customers that *they feel like you feel* about your product or service. Notice that I said: *Feel . . .* I did not say think.

When developing leadership, it takes 'will power' mixed with just the right amount of 'want power' to create a leader. A key element in my personal success is the way I was raised, having grown up with eleven brothers and sisters. My family replayed success continually like a broken LP record does when it's at the end of the song — circling again and again. As a fifth grader I applied for the position of altar boy at our church as did my friends. Each boy had to complete the memory work within the customary two week deadline without any special dispensation. My friends finished their assignments by the deadline, but I was not able to complete mine because I could not memorize the material within two weeks. I had a speech impediment which slowed me down, but I was determined to become an altar boy anyway. Father Crosier could see determination and passion in my eyes and sent me a copy of the memory work with instructions to start early for next year. He gave me another chance. This meant I would compete with boys a year younger, but that did not negate my desire to become an altar boy. I started learning the material immediately, and by the end of the next year I was assisting every priest on the altar. I was taught to build on success and use failure positively. My parents used the old adage, "Try, try again." I studied twice as long as the other members of my altar boy graduating class, and I succeeded because I did not dwell on personal failure. Too often, we over-dramatize our failures instead of using the positives to overshadow the negatives.

Prior to having a meeting with your fellow team members, think of some of the successes the team has shared in the past, and relive them verbally. About ten years ago there was a football player at the University of Georgia named Herschel Walker. The football coaches have every person who makes the team watch a film of Herschel Walker running touchdowns between the prickly hedges at the university. Why?

A picture of success is sometimes best remembered without words. A picture is clearly worth a thousand words as the cliche goes, and the picture Herschel Walker painted of success and leadership is long remembered by the University of Georgia football team. Also, every football player at Georgia sees his incredible enthusiasm on the field, and his enthusiasm has been contagious. Write the word enthusiasm on a piece of paper. E N T H U S I A S M. Underline I A S M. It stands for — I Am Sold Myself. If you want to develop into a successful leader, then sell yourself. Remember, enthusiasm counts — whether you're running with a football down the field or leading your internal team.

Another important aspect of becoming a leader is the desire to find a model of excellence — someone who is doing the right thing consistently. Such a person has his or her life in perfect balance emotionally, spiritually, physically and financially. Dick Biggs, a member of the Georgia Speakers Association, wrote a book called, *If Life is a Balancing Act, Why Am I So Darn Clumsy?*. His message is simple: if you want to be a leader, improve yourself. Whom do you know who exemplifies a great model of excellence for patterning your life? If you cannot find a personal friend, business colleague, or family member, then find someone — maybe a politician, a philospher, a pastor, or a priest. An anonymous person once said, "Follow what wise men do and do what they do, and you, too, shall be a wise man." Be confident, enthusiastic, and completely committed in whatever you do.

If you embrace the following tips, they will help you to develop your team:

Our success is often presupposed by our clothing. People prejudge someone by the clothing he or she wears. Although wearing fine-quality clothing usually indicates success, you should make the most of your money. Wear the best clothes you can afford. Not all of us are rolling in money. However discount department stores offer substantial savings on name-brand designer clothing. Likewise, gray duct tape around the shoe is unacceptable, and a safety pin which hinges an ear piece onto a frame of a pair of glasses screams "Unsuccessful!" Most people feel someone is unsuccessful if his or her appearance is in disarray. Leaders want their team members to dress successfully because customers expect it.

Wear a smile. A smile requires only seven muscles; a frown requires twenty-eight. How many people do you know are working overtime with only their faces?

Eye-contact is important to customers. Look a person directly in the eye. Also *make sure your handshake is a normal handshake.* Do not use a two-handed handshake, which is actually an action of physical control and is not considered friendly when used in business. If a female and male are standing together and you are introduced, *make sure you shake the woman's hand first* and then the man's hand. Whether a pair of customers are married or not married, you might alienate a potential female buyer by assuming the man is going to be the buyer. So often in the automobile industry, in particular, the sale of a car is blown because the sales person greets the male customer before greeting the female.

Great salespeople are not born; they learn by set behavior patterns which respond to what people really want. People want recognition, love, money, respect, satisfaction, security, help, peace of mind, intimacy, status, success and happiness. These are the same needs that your team has. Your team needs love, money, respect, satisfaction, security, success, happiness, and so forth, just like the customers do. These needs motivate and inspire people on your team to develop from within so they will not fail.

How can you give these qualities to your team? For one, I use humor in seminars when I feel the atmospheric pressure needs to be lightened. I tell them most of our customers listen to the same radio station — W I I F M. The call letters of this station are What's In It For Me. That's selfish. I suggest leaders rather use the four C's to leadership: *conversation, common ground, care* and *compassion.*

Do you want the internal customer to listen to you? If so, listen to your team constantly, and use *conversation* to develop a successful team by developing the leaders within them. Internal and external customers listen to each other. Conversely, if you want them to listen to you, then you must be willing to listen to them first. Listening is reciprocal.

Making use of visual and verbal vocal systems, I show a variety of props when I teach a group on leadership. My props include different hats, a tiny shoe that says "I like to put my foot in the door" and a pre-scription pad designed for a doctor — props and promotional pieces that ensure the group remembers me from the masses and that we have a common ground, or common bond, of doing business together. I hand out little stones by the hundreds that remind us also to leave "no stone unturned." In the meeting room, there's a gigantic picture of my feet that says, "We will knock your socks off." The sign is hard to miss. . . but my feet are not. People buy emotionally, and they justify through logic. Since they do, we need to show our team members the benefits of working together; if they work constructively together as internal cus-tomers, without a doubt they will take care of the external customers — with little effort.

Dennis Swanberg's book, *Is Your Love Tank Full?,* captures my thoughts perfectly. Dennis is a writer and gifted comedian who delivers his material on his television show with such flavor and enthusiasm that every audience enjoys his tasteful comedic view of family and spousal relationships, and he does this using voice changes and foreign accents. Before you know it he has the audience quartered and wrapped for display, but you do not care. It takes sincerity and *caring* to show someone how to improve himself. Swanberg says in his book, *Is Your Love Tank Full?,* "Don't let your yesterdays take too much of your todays." Often we dwell on yesterday's failures, troubles, and headaches so much that these trials dominate too much of our daily work. Do you let that happen to you? A leader learns to use these lessons of life that turn failure and disappointment into stepping stones of successful leadership; his internal customers learn from him, duplicating the process for the external customer.

If you do not want to use the word *compassion* then use *compliment.* *Compliment* your team. Everyone loves to be appreciated and acknowl-edged for a job well done. Start now by recognizing your performers.

Delight your customers and continuously improve your customer relationships. The road to success is always under construction. Unfortunately, even though it takes months to create a smoothly paved road, construction of a roadway is not completed once the workers load their equipment into trucks and ride away. The effects of weather, automobile accidents and constant usage cause the road to erode. A leader cannot have a smooth ride to success without patching problems that arise, correcting mistakes or even sometimes completely overhauling the sales team. We must keep a constant lookout for improvement. If the going gets easy, you may be coasting downhill. The uphill climb, however, brings the leader in closer toward success with customers.

Delighting your internal customer and watching your external customers blossom will not happen without developing the leader within you first. Concentrate on yourself. See you on the road to success!

My Prescription for Leadership
by D.J. Harrington

• Give your team support from someone who counts — you
• Help them assess their abilities honestly
• Provide them with training necessary for learning their jobs
• Make sure your team realizes you are actually working for them
• Compliment your people as often as possible
• Motivate your team to change, if necessary
• Show them how to treat the external customer by treating them like customers
• Teach them the importance of overcoming mistakes, and provide them with constructive ways to change, if necessary
• Show them the importance of working constructively as a team

ABOUT
D.J. HARRINGTON

D.J. Harrington is President and Chief Executive Officer of Phone Logic, Inc., an international telemarketing and training company based in Atlanta, GA. Harrington serves as a consultant to over 600 privately owned businesses throughout the U.S., training personnel at all levels — from operators, customer service representatives, sales staff to president of the company. He's a true believer in selling as a science. World-wide, D.J. has provided clients with marketing and telephone skills designed to enhance and improve their sales techniques. He believes that by using a scientific method of behavior modification, people become successful with customers when they work on the self issue first.

D.J. received his degree from St. Leo College in 1970. His spectacular delivery and expertise in speaking has earned him the #1 rating at the national Automobile Dealers Association convention (twice), at the National Autobody Convention and Exposition, as well as in the carpet and real estate industries. A syndicated columnist for 33 newspapers, D.J. is featured weekly on ASTN, the national training network. He is co-author of another book, Reach for the Stars.

Contact information:
Phone Logic, Inc.
2820 Andover Way
Woodstock, GA 30189
℡ (770) 924-4400
fax (770) 516-7797
℡ (800) 552-5252
e-mail: djharrington@mindspring.com

WHAT DID I SEE YOU SAY?

"The most important thing in communication
is to hear what isn't being said." — Peter Drucker

by Larry Leger

There are over 3,000 books in print with "leader" in the title, and they are increasing in number as you read this chapter. Current labels and buzzwords delineating leadership and management styles for the millennium ebb and flow, with the most recent tidal wave stirred up by the latest management guru with more degrees than a thermometer. The essential fundamentals are still in there somewhere, and, if we are discriminating, we will sift the sands of information and opinion and find that of value which fits our needs. Philosophically, leadership is action based on belief. Pragmatically, leadership will always be dependent on knowing where we want to go and what we want to achieve and on utilizing interpersonal skills to direct our resources of people, products and profit to take the action to succeed.

Every leader has a distinctive style — a trademark as unique as any product brand or company logo. Acceptable styles are evolving from the dictatorial "my way or the highway" of yesterday to the interactive "do, demonstrate, delegate" model of today. Followers are more educated, experienced and thus more demanding that leaders be proactive to be in a position to give direction, to facilitate actions, to evaluate progress and to celebrate success. The product or service is irrelevant. Universally we are all sellers and buyers. To be a true leader we must sell ourselves and our basic philosophy to attract and inspire followers, who in reality are participants. Everyone has a role to play, and even these roles are in flux and often interchangeable. It is no accident that one of the currently touted organization models, the *team*, is an acronym for *T*ogether *W*e *A*chieve *M*ore. Interaction is imperative to achievement in any venture, project or business. The strategy has changed from overpower to empower.

In most of those 3,000+ books on leadership and management, we read about what can be summarized into the "C" attributes of leadership: Committed, Consistent, Competent, Competitive, Convincing, Confident, Candid, Courageous, Caring, Considerate, Compassionate, Concise, Charismatic . . . and always Communicative.

Let's focus on the term "Communicative." No one has to be convinced of the importance of this attribute. Communication skills are interwoven into every aspect of leadership. Successful communication gets others to sign on to our agendas. Communication by its very definition includes non-verbal as well as verbal components. It is "the act of transmitting" or "giving or exchanging of information, signals or messages by talk, gestures, writing. . . ." Most of our attention is directed to written and verbal forms of getting our messages out. These basic forms of exchange are vital to sharing information, providing guidelines, establishing goals and priorities and evaluating progress and achievement.

I believe there are two communicative formats to which we should give serious attention. One generally touched on, but not fully developed, is listening, a topic worthy of a chapter of its own and a skill we should all give more attention and practice. The other is given an occasional reference but seldom identified as a separate skill and certainly not assigned its due importance to the complex process of communication. This somewhat neglected format is the non-verbal communication of body language. Body language, or more scientifically termed kinesis, communicates an imperative message. At the very least, it communicates image, emotions and attitudes essential to understanding.

Margot Robinson, author of *Egos and Eggshells*, equates much of non-verbal communication with the smoke signals of the early Native Americans and describes them as "hazy, coded, non-verbal messages that are not easy to decipher." And most likely she is correct; however, I would wager that you know a great deal more about body language and its myriad of signals than you realize. Let's start with the odds that you would agree with the adage, "Actions speak louder than words." How about, "Don't let them see you sweat," "I can read her like a book," "We got our signals crossed," "If looks could kill," or "From across the room he undressed her with his eyes." Did I score any points?

Ed Bauer, author of *Communicative Techniques for Today's Manager*, begins his list of the "13 Attributes of the Successful Manager" with, "Understand body language and use it." In other words, pay attention to the non-verbal signals and turn them to your advantage. Everything is judged by appearance. What is not specifically articulated or communicated visually counts for nothing. Communicating is something you do with your entire body all the time. Like the Hawaiian hula, every little movement has a meaning all its own!

We certainly appreciate and value first impressions, physical appearance, handshakes, speech patterns and tone, grammar, poise and eye contact. Everyone and everything communicates, be it material objects, physical space, time systems, speech, print, clothes . . . and body language. You do know more than you realize. If we were in a group setting I would have you perform a recognizable bit of body language. In the average group, there would be many obvious examples — and perhaps a few surprises. Let's picture handshakes, pats on the back, fists shaken, stares, smiles, winks, pointed fingers, waves, exaggerated postures and so on. Or try this exercise; turn the volume off on the television and see if you still get the gist of the plot. Bet you did!

Body language is both old and new. Primitive man communicated without a spoken or written language. In the first century A.D. the Roman teacher of oratory, Marcus Fabius, argued that gestures should enhance the impact of the spoken word. Shakespeare said, "There language in her eye, her cheek, her lip, Nay her foot speaks; her wanton

spirits leak out at every joint and motion of her body." Emerson con-
curred with, "The eyes of men converse as much as their tongues" and
in the Bible we read in Proverbs, "He winketh with his eyes, he speaketh
with his feet, he teacheth with his fingers." Sammy Cahn's song lyrics
tell us that "there's a kind of walk you walk when the world's outdone
you" and Olivia Newton-John asked to "let me hear your body talk" and
what mother has never demanded "Look at me when I talk to you!"
Even Earl K. Long, the famous and infamous legend in Louisiana
politics, knew how to use body language. He has been quoted as saying,
"Don't write anything you can phone, don't phone anything you can talk
face to face, don't talk anything you can smile, don't smile anything you
can wink and don't wink anything you can nod."

Scientific interest in body language became considerable between
1914 and 1940 and serious study developed in the 1950's, spurred
somewhat by public interest. Julius Fast, popular author and proponent
of body language, contends that every movement — the way we stand,
sit, walk, cross our legs, use our eyes or move our hand — offers clues
to unconscious motive and meanings. Dr. Ray L. Birdwhistell, credited
inventor of the science of kinesis, defines it as the systematic study of
how humans communicate through body movement and gestures. He has
said, "Man is a multi-sensorial being — occasionally he verbalizes."
Faster than you can speak, your body sends a message, and you receive
immediate feedback from your audience, be it one person or many.

As humans, we all use body language and read or misread it without
much thought. Most of us have intuitively interpreted non-verbal
messages all our life. As the research gives us greater understanding of
this complex form of communication, it behooves us to utilize our
knowledge to produce the reactions we desire and to react and respond
to the real messages from others. Consider the value! Statistics vary in
analyzing message impact. On the average, indications are that messages
are 7% verbal — choice of words; 38% vocal — tone of voice; 55% body
language. Many estimates are as high as 80% non-verbal. Can we afford
to misread — or worse, to ignore these messages? I think not! We know

body language is vital to first impressions. Before you say anything, people have already made a decision on some level as to whether or not they will listen to you or give credibility to what you say.

Individuals engage in non-verbal communication, not basically to be clever or devious, but because these means of communicating are deeply embedded in the habits of man and automatically transmitted by all cultures. We tend to develop the body language of the culture of the language which we speak. Bilingual languages equate to bilingual body language. The science of body language is extremely complex. It is estimated that the human body is capable of assuming about one thousand different positions and about 20,000 facial expressions . . . and you have seen most of them in the workplace! Dr. Paul Ekman has classified over 7,000 facial expressions in over ten years of study and mastered most of them himself. The average person can demonstrate four eyebrow movements, four eyelid movements, seven mouth positions and three ways to nod. Try it. Those expressions most easily recognizable and crossing cultural lines are sadness, happiness, anger, surprise and disgust — every actor's stock in trade. And they can be yours for the taking.

"Reading" body language is as important as it is complicated. Most of us do not wish to be misunderstood, nor to misunderstand; we do not wish to insult, nor to appear stupid, insensitive or crude to others. A word of caution — there are no absolutes in body language and no simple, foolproof code. We may cite examples and make generalizations. We must be aware of the many forms and components of body language — the context of the situation, the expectations of the performance and, outside our own sphere of geography, the cultural differences, especially of space and time.

Let us look briefly at facial expression and eye movement. You have a whole repertoire of signals — eyes that meet and hold another's in defiance — testing authority or dominance to eyes that say, "I find you interesting." Normal eye contact is one second. Eyes can threaten, frighten, hate, love, seduce, ignore, plead or reproach — without a single word being spoken. They can express confidence, depression, guilt, forgiveness, or evasiveness. Notice any teenagers, or staff, "roll" their eyes lately? Anyone give or receive any "dirty looks" or experience any "non-person" treatment? Our eyebrows speak volumes, sometimes unconsciously. A friend of mine relates a story from her first teaching position. It seems that one afternoon she overheard two students outside the classroom discussing whether she was "in a good mood" today. While listening to hear the response, she was surprised to learn that these students, and likely more of them, had determined that verbal instructions to quiet down and/or get to work were more serious if she raised her right eyebrow when delivering such instruction. Unaware that she did this, she began to realize that the observation was indeed true. Now in a management position with adult employees, she tells me that to this day she uses this non-verbal tool to her advantage!

Our facial expressions are our most readily observed body language, with smiles and other mouth gestures most prevalent: Happy smiles, acknowledgment smiles, laughing smiles, apologetic smiles, polite smiles and even a smirk or sneer. My personal favorite is the "I've got a secret" or the "I know something you are dying to know" smile. The South is generally a high smile area; New England, a low smile area. All is not positive. We can observe the depression droop, the set jaw "you ain't changing my mind". . . and on to spitting — considered as aggressive and uncouth; showing contempt or disgust — much akin to sticking out one's tongue. Do you remember the song lyric, "Your lips say no, no; but your eyes say yes, yes?" Perhaps this interpretation, although likely invalid, may have an implication in instances of harassment charges, reinforcing the need to use all the signals of communication instead of jumping to conclusions based on one signal.

We have less conscious control over our hands, arms and legs. Stress and anxiety can slip out despite facial control. Confidence or doubt are commonly evidenced by steepling one's hands — watch a political talk show. Rubbing the nose is usually a qualifier, generally indicating a negative. Covering the mouth happens when we would rather not talk, when we said something we think we should not have said or when we are surprised — watch a TV game show or beauty pageant. Law enforcement generally agrees that this gesture communicates a wide range of emotions from self-doubt to lying. Other signs of doubt are rubbing beside the ear or eye and nose pinching. Shrugs are generally characterized as negative — either "I don't know, I'm not interested or I don't care."

We tend to complicate our interactions with barriers: One such typical barrier is the closed posture with folded arms; others are pointing fingers or turning the body away. Barriers vary with position and degree of resistance. Body movements can contradict what we say — from tapping fingers to shuffling feet, from tightly locking the ankles to leaning toward or away from another. Those arguing will not take the same positions; they will assume opposite positions. Observers will take the position of those with whom they agree. Mirror imaging can help to make a subordinate feel comfortable or even disarm an opponent who is attempting to intimidate.

Again, be cautious about becoming an immediate expert. There are contradictions in interpreting body language. For example, fidgeters in an audience are assumed to be bored. Maybe, but they may be tired, sleepy, uncomfortable, preoccupied, hyper, fearful, or suffering from underwear that is too tight! No body posture or movement by itself has a precise meaning. Psychologist Marianne La Franco of Boston College says that body language is too complex to fake convincingly for any length of time. Some highly successful poker players made great strides in this direction.

Body language and the spoken word depend on each other. If you listen to one and not to the other you, will receive a distorted message. You can stop talking, but you cannot stop communicating. You either say the right or the wrong thing — you cannot say nothing. Usually we tend to fit in or use the body language and gestures expected of us in a given situation — social, work, school, recreational. We all know something about the vocabulary of body symbols. Watch an impersonator, or ask almost any employee or student to mimic a boss or teacher. The results are revealing!

Dr. Edward T. Hall, professor of anthropology at Northwestern University and renowned author, has treated a most fascinating aspect of body language — our use of space. Hall has broken distance for communication into four zones — intimate, personal, social and public. Space has great implications for meetings, classroom management, work and personal relationships. Intimate is close enough to touch — up to eighteen inches — good with lovers, good friends, children and parents. Personal space zones are one and one half to four feet — you can touch, but don't have to. An example is two people who want privacy within a group. This can create a "bubble" or protective sphere. Violation of space is threatening, especially in public places. You can readily observe this space zone violated or threatened in an elevator. If you really want to create anxiety — face someone in an elevator and heaven forbid, speak! Social space is usually four to twelve feet and is used to transact impersonal business — to meet repairmen, to lecture. It is an average work distance — eye contact can be greater without risk of embarrassment. Public space is twelve feet plus and deals with performance — it is easy to "act," to exaggerate body language to convey message and is much less personal. The greater the distance, the less one-to-one communication — one can "hide" or blend. We generally refer to acceptable use of space as our "comfort zones."

Add to this need to control our space our differences in personality and nationality, and we greatly increase the complexity of the matter. Consider the introvert versus the extrovert, levels of maturity and life experiences, race, cultural heritage, education and gender, to name the more obvious differences. For a simplified example, examine gender space in your next meeting. Posture gives some indication of confidence and authority. Males tend to expand and occupy more space merely with posture and gestures. Females tend to close and confine space. Credibility and authority can be enhanced by "filling the space" and positioning. Observe the individual who comes into a group or room and makes his or her presence felt. Immediately one has a sense of leadership provided only by body language — erect posture, a look of confidence, eye contact, a smile, projection of energy, ease of movement and gesture. We characterize this by saying that he or she has a commanding presence. This individual has yet to speak and we are ready to listen and likely believe. We can all develop this use of body language and use it to our advantage.

People very seldom say what they actually think. They seldom express true feelings and desires in words . . . we mask, we hedge, we say what is expected, we qualify. Yet we all reveal ourselves in the way we hold our bodies, use our facial muscles, gesture and touch. We telegraph our thoughts and feelings with physical signals. As leaders we should hone the skill to read body language and to receive information and attitude; to project an image; to model expectation; to control a negotiation; to root out the real issue; to evaluate the feedback and to define a course of action. Change is inevitable and constant. Growth is a matter of choice. Listen with your eyes.

Happy People Watching! — Yogi Berra

ABOUT
LARRY LEGER

*L*arry Leger is a thirty-year veteran of the automotive industry. He is president and Chief Operating Officer of American Management Service, located in the heart of Cajun Country in south Louisiana. He is as pure Cajun as you're ever going to meet; he speaks the language and enjoys his hobby of cooking good ole spicy Cajun food.

Larry is one of the most requested consultants and motivational speakers in the automotive industry, presenting at many national and international conventions. A true hands-on consultant with the re-engineering skills sought by many, he clearly is the definition of the "Roads Scholar." His speaking career has brought him to every state in the U.S. and to other countries.

Contact information:
American Management Service
P.O. Box L
Grand Coteau, LA 70541-1011
✆ (800) 992-2920
fax (318) 662-7242

LEADING BY CONVICTION — RAISING SUCCESS TO SIGNIFICANCE

by Lisa Jimenez, M.Ed.

Courage. Focus. Vision. Dedication. Confidence. Commitment.

These are some of the qualities that all good leaders have. Right? Yes. Good leaders have most of these qualities. And some would argue that good leaders might also have some good luck. But, in fact, this list of qualities is probably just the beginning.

What is the essential quality that makes great leaders? — exceptional leaders? — like the kind who turn a bankrupt company into a million-dollar venture; great leaders — like the kind who change a world's beliefs and promote freedom for countries in bondage; great leaders — like the kind who turn a rebellious teenager into a well-mannered young man or woman. You won't see these on CNN, but their home videos would make an inspiring documentary. Of all the leaders I have interviewed and studied, I found one common attribute in every one. Great leaders have all mastered this one core quality. This master quality is what fosters all other leadership qualities. This quality is CONVICTION.

It is conviction — total belief in themselves, their company and the people they lead. It is conviction that separates good leaders from great leaders. Webster defines conviction as strong belief and confidence. (The justice system defines conviction as a successful trial, but even those great prosecutors need Webster's definition of conviction to do their job.) It is through a strong conviction that all the other qualities of good leadership come out. Conviction fosters incredible courage, laser focus, passion and an empowering vision.

All great leaders have conviction and the ability to convey that conviction in a way that empowers the people they lead.

Great leaders lead by this main principle. Their leadership comes from the heart. Decisions are made with the head but conviction is made with the heart. Their leadership is Spirit driven. They are not just interested in success or being successful. They are concerned with who they become and who they help develop along the way. Great leaders are interested not just in success, but in significance. Their conviction involves how they can develop the individual and themselves. You see, with conviction you never have to worry about contradiction. The two cannot co-exist!

I experienced the power of conviction while writing my book, *Conquer Fear! Ending Procrastination and Self-Sabotage to Achieve What You Really Want.* I began this writing project knowing that this book was needed mainly because I needed it. And I knew I wasn't the only one having this problem. I had planned to survey all of my friends and family to see if they were also experiencing it; but, well, I kept procrastinating. Finally, I searched for all the information I could on the subject of fear, faith and procrastination. After reading several books and countless periodicals, I came up with a tangible way to find out why we procrastinate and how to solve it. So, I began to write.

My writing reflected all the research and all of my "head knowledge" I've accumulated through my degrees in psychology and education. Well, when I had nearly finished writing the book, I reread what I had written. It was good. Pretty darn good. But it wasn't great. Something was missing. It had all the "head knowledge" anyone would ever need to break through the procrastination habit. But it was lacking that something special. The book was lacking conviction. And, I think a reader can smell a lack of conviction in the same way a horse can smell fear.

I did the only thing I knew how to do. I prayed. I looked into my soul and pulled out the answer. It came. I realized that the book was speaking from the head only. It wasn't speaking from the heart. Immediately I got out a pad of paper and began to write from the heart. I discovered a whole new reason for procrastination — the truth about procrastination. It was in line with my relationship with my soul. I began writing with a heart perspective. All my life I had been told, "Never be afraid of hard work." Perhaps I had just heard wrong, and it was actually "Never be afraid of heart work," because that was the secret. I found conviction that the book was missing.

I knew then that the book project wouldn't just have an effect on the present. It could have an affect on eternity. It had significance. When I added the writing from that level of consciousness to the first draft (the head), I had found the missing link. (And here I had always thought the "missing link" was some kind of monster. On the contrary — it was beautiful.) The book now had conviction. Instantaneously, I had a strong vision of how, where, when and to whom I would market this book. The project became easier, clearer and more fun. I had a high purpose, a mission behind the project. It all came out of conviction. Through that experience I discovered first-hand how conviction fosters laser focus, passion, incredible courage and a strong sense of vision.

Seek your soul. There lie your purpose and your conviction. Not only will you help yourself find true life-fulfillment, but you will also serve others in the most powerful, effective way possible — authentically and boldly! You must first know yourself. And that may not come easily for some people. But you must take the time necessary for the introspective thinking needed to do so. Only you can do it . . . there is no shortcut, there is no "Soul-searching for Dummies" book available. But once you know who you are, you can build on where you want to go. When you search your soul for your unique conviction, and communicate that conviction in your leadership role, it is then that you can touch other people's souls. What a powerful, fulfilling privilege. Bring your convictions to your workplace. Incorporate your conviction in your leadership role. It is by conviction you will attain all the other qualities needed for successful leadership. Great leaders have conviction. Conviction comes out of your soul. Seek your soul.

All great leaders have conviction and the ability to convey that conviction in a way that empowers the people they lead.

All meaningful change starts from within. Whether you are a leader of a company, an association, a country, or a family, the same principles apply. You need to begin your mission from within by setting your personal standard of excellence. You must work on yourself before you work on those you lead. Great leaders get the results they do because they begin with their own behaviors. They know that every great success precedes a personal success. All major success follows success in your personal growth. And great leaders do not walk around loudly announcing these behavioral changes they've made. They just make the changes quietly — inwardly, and then "walk their talk." But those they lead will notice. Expect change in yourself before you expect change in others.

"But it's so tough to make changes," you might say. Or, "This is just how I am." Making changes is hard to do. We sometimes resist changes like a child resists spinach. (OK, perhaps an adult, too.)

But not making changes is even harder because it leads to frustration and failure. Out of conviction comes the courage to make the changes necessary for success. Great leaders know that the choices they make frame the very essence of who they are. This truth can give you the desire and the courage to make changes in yourself before expecting change in others.

I experienced this truth when my husband, Mark, was complaining about the fifteen employees in our alarm business. We had been in business for almost a year. The company was doing okay but the employees were not performing as they should. "They don't show up for our meetings." Mark complained. "Most of them come to work late and then don't know what to do when they get there." After listening to all these woes, I suggested we create an employee manual with each employee's job description and expectations. (Even though we had been in business for a year, we had never done this.) We spent many hours that weekend putting this employee manual together. It was a beauty — complete with four-color graphics! I was so proud of it; I even thought we could sell it to other companies. Or maybe it belonged on the shelves at Barnes & Noble.

Mark announced there would be a special meeting first thing Monday morning. He ran into the meeting room (a few minutes late) and began to hand out the colorful manuals. "I have put together a list of job descriptions and expectations for each one of you," he began. "This manual will help make us a better company. Good luck, everyone." The fifteen employees walked out of the meeting room, spiffy manual in hand, without a word.

A few minutes later, Mark got his keys and started heading out of the building. As he walked towards the parking lot, something caught his eye. Something was dangling from a branch of the large oak tree outside his office. And it was on fire! Mark rushed over and did his best Smoky the Bear impression, batting away the last of the flames. What had been burning? A copy of his beautiful four-color employee manual, now simply charcoal and black. And, undoubtedly, unread in the few minutes that had passed since he had handed them out. Perhaps like Moses and the burning bush, there was a message here too.

Like many new businesses, we made many mistakes when we started our company thirteen years ago. These colossal mistakes caused us to go on a search for knowledge about great leadership. But I am convinced we would not have been able to turn that company into the million dollar company it is unless we had been willing to make the changes in ourselves before expecting them in our employees. The conviction we had to serve others, and to create a great company, fueled our desire to change and to become experts at leading others.

The biggest mistakes we made were that we had no clear mission and conviction concerning our company or our employees. They could never buy into this new employee manual because it didn't reflect our core values, our beliefs or our conviction. It couldn't reflect them, because at that time we didn't even know our core values, beliefs or convictions! The other mistake was expecting change in our employees' behaviors before first expecting it in ourselves. We would never get the behaviors we wanted — or the results we wanted from our employees — until we started making some changes in our own behaviors.

We began to take responsibility for our education by reading, interviewing and studying the art of leadership. (Not to be confused with the "leadership of art" which centers on famous painters from the 1600's.) We began the process of changing our own behaviors. An amazing thing began to happen. When we took responsibility for our own behaviors, we saw tremendous change in our employees. The hidden gem in all this is that as soon as you set your standards and your beliefs, you begin getting what you want — greater results in your people — which causes those very beliefs to be strengthened. We made the transition from "Belief" to "Relief" very quickly.

I challenge you to work on yourself first. All meaningful change begins from within. Expect change in yourself before you expect change in others. Do the introspective work needed to take an honest assessment of your talents and your weaknesses. This isn't always easy. (Feel free to take two aspirin before beginning the process.) Make the changes needed in your own abilities or delegate the responsibility to someone else who can do what you want. Great leaders get the results they get because they begin with their own behaviors.

List your 5 strongest leadership qualities: _____,

_____, _____, _____,

_____.

List your 5 weakest leadership qualities _____,

_____, _____, _____,

_____.

Decide which of these qualities you choose to delegate to others and which of these behaviors you choose to change in yourself.

How do you change behaviors? Now, that's a great question! There is a great answer. And it's a simple one. But it's an answer worth every penny you paid for this book. You change your behaviors by changing your beliefs.

"Change your beliefs — and you change your behaviors. Change your behaviors — and you change your results. Change your results — and you change your life."

That is my signature statement that I live my life by and convey to all my audiences — and to everyone I meet. It is a powerful truth. Your beliefs cause your behaviors. You can change your behaviors by changing the beliefs that cause them.

The first step is to know that you have power over your beliefs. Beliefs are like jackets — if they don't serve you, you can take them off and change them! The most challenging part about negative beliefs is that most of the time you aren't even aware of them. You don't see how they hurt you or even destroy you. But others do. To accomplish change, you must have a B.A. Don't worry, you can get a B.A. without ever going to college. A 'B.A.' is a "Belief Assessment." You must take the time to honestly assess your beliefs, positive and negative, in order to change them. Negative belief barriers are one of the biggest killers of successful leadership. This explains why some people achieve their goals, while others take the same goal-setting class, setting the goals they say they want, and still don't accomplish them. Ultimately, procrastination and self-sabotage creep in. These cripple your leadership efforts because you don't stand for anything or you have negative beliefs that choke your potential. But when you can step back, and recognize these factors that are limiting you, you can have amazing personal breakthroughs.

Several years ago, while attending a National Speakers Association conference in Bermuda, I faced one of those life-changing breakthroughs. Like most people at the conference, I was inspired by all the great information and fired up about all the possibilities that lie ahead in my career . . . or so I thought. My friend and business coach, Randy Gage, and I were talking together about building my speaking business.

"You could speak to XYZ Company." My friend Randy said.

"No." I replied. "I'm better with different types of audiences than that."

"Okay." He replied and went on, "Your fee should be at $___ and you could market to ABC industry."

"No. I don't think I'm ready for that." I quickly said. "I have three children and a husband who isn't too supportive of this career."

I found myself starting to sweat, and was sure it was the hot Bermuda sun. After several of these responses Randy looked at me and said, "Lisa, you are afraid of success!"

Now, what would your reply be to someone who accuses you of being afraid of success? Yep! You guessed it. I argued, "No, I'm not! What do you know anyway? You don't even have children."

Well, Randy is the kind of friend who knows how to read between words and has the courage to tell you what he sees. So he repeated, "You're afraid of really making it in this business." After pondering that statement for a long time, I knew he was right. And, boy, can the truth hurt sometimes. Those words struck a painful cord in me and there's no Band-Aid big enough to cover that kind of wound. And, being in Bermuda, I couldn't just rush out to the mall and buy a new pair of shoes to forget about it.

No, the truth broke me that day and I began to say aloud all the reasons why I was afraid of really making it in this career . . . Would I be a good mother with the demands of a successful career? Who was I to think I could accomplish such great success? After all, I grew up in the era when girls were seen and not heard. I'm too young. I'm too inexperienced. And the one insecurity that every successful person encounters from time to time — no matter how irrational — I'm nothing but a fraud and I'm going to be found out! That day, I realized I had been allowing those negative beliefs to choke my potential and limit my success. I knew I was in need of some introspective, soul-searching decisions about my career and my beliefs.

What about you? What are your negative belief barriers? Do you ever say,

"I'm too old."

"I'm too young."

"Men never change."

"Money is evil."

"I can't save."

"Everyone will laugh."

"I'm not good enough."

"We can't do it this way."

"A woman can't be a leader."

"Chocolate is bad."

"What will the neighbors think?"

"What will mom and dad think?"

If you have any of these negative belief barriers, your behavior will actually repel opportunity. It will just push it away, like it's the spinach. More often than not, people do not take advantage of opportunity simply because they are not aware of it — or it is not congruent with their beliefs. So they don't respond to the opportunities or they're just not aware of them. They have just tuned them out the way people tune out commercials while watching television. (Personally, I have learned how to tune out the entire Jerry Springer Show, even while having it blare at me in my doctor's waiting room.)

The following action steps will help you identify your self-limiting beliefs to help you become the leader you were meant to be and help you empower others to break through their own belief barriers. I challenge you to look at the hidden message that your behavior is screaming out.

1. Identify self-limiting beliefs.

Later that day in Bermuda I did an exercise that changed my career. I took out a sheet of paper and wrote the word "Millionaire" across the top of the page. Then I listed all the connotations I had in my belief system to that word. What came out shocked me . . .

I wrote things like, millionaires are selfish. Millionaires are so busy they aren't good parents. "Where did this come from?" I yelled! The reason I was having difficulty became obvious. My subconscious was actually repelling success in order to protect me. Why? Because of all those negative beliefs and pain I had connected to achieving that goal. I linked too much pain to achieving my goal. It wasn't just like a lightbulb going off in my head; it was like an entire fourth of July fireworks display. The "oohs" and "ahhs" became a glorious "Aha!" Breaking through, I realized the need to take steps to change those beliefs.

I began by calling my husband from Bermuda and shared all my fears and reasons I had not allowed myself to move forward. His response was, "Thank God you finally see it!" When I returned home, I stepped off the plane to him holding a bouquet of flowers and a card that read, "Now, let's get to work!" It was one of those teary airport scenes we've all seen a million times (and, admittedly, were curious about what the people's story was). I wanted to shout out loud, "You're right, honey, let's do it, let's get to work," but I was afraid that we would be escorted out by airport security. But, I happily realized he wasn't the uncaring tyrant I had accused him of being (or wanted him to be).

2. Create positive connotations to your goal.

When I returned to work, I knew it was imperative for me to work at changing my beliefs about success. I had to attach positive connotations to being successful. I wrote down every example I knew of successful people helping others and using their success for a power of good. I posted a personal quote that I began living my life by:

- Change your beliefs and you change your behaviors.
- Change your behaviors and you change your results.

I completed the breakthrough I began in Bermuda with the following exercise. I wrote down on a sheet of paper all the positive connotations I could think of to success. I could help my church spread the Gospel. I could help an aspiring speaker. I could travel with my family and teach my children all about the different cultures. The one possibility that stirred me the most was, I could treat my mom to a vacation in Hawaii . . . just the two of us!

As soon as I changed those beliefs and attached positive connotations to my goal of being a successful speaker, my career soared. I used the power of vision to keep me motivated on a daily basis. I began collecting inspiring quotes about the choices money could give me and pasting pictures of the places we wanted to visit, and thought of the foundations I could help support. I even placed the outfit I was going to wear to Hawaii outside my closet (which also kept me in great physical shape, as I didn't want to achieve my goal and then not fit into the dress!).

Just eight months after that life-changing breakthrough, I had more dates on my calendar than I have ever had in my career. It was a great feeling when I gave my church enough money to help them buy cappuccino machines for their college ministry. It was fun sending money to people (sometimes anonymously) at a time when I knew they could really use it. But, the best feeling of all was wearing that outfit — that hung outside my closet for so long — on the airplane and spending five incredible days with my mom in Hawaii! I had traveled thousands of miles from Bermuda to Hawaii, both literally and figuratively.

Have you ever received a lead or contact only to lose it due to lack of follow-up? Do you ever find yourself hurting your chances of moving ahead by misplacing an important file, being late to an appointment or not returning a prospect's phone call? This amazing, simple, two-part breakthrough really can change your life. The mind is a remarkable tool and, when mixed with the right beliefs and conviction, the charge is unstoppable. Most people don't even realize they have self-limiting beliefs and that these beliefs are choking their potential. You can evaluate your beliefs by your behaviors. These behaviors could be wake-up calls for you to evaluate your belief system. You may be holding on to self-limiting beliefs.

The final truth I want to leave you with is that this is a process. Great leadership evolves. Give yourself and others the time to develop. And when you are faced with a time of burnout and you find yourself tired of the process, remember my Success Cycle Principle: *Success is a cycle of enthusiasm and discipline.*

The cycle of success is like the recycling symbol. It has arrows moving clockwise. The arrows represent enthusiasm and discipline. Both are needed in the equation of success. I've never been much of a math wizard, but this is one equation that is simple. All successes are fueled by enthusiasm. It's contagious! Enthusiasm helps you accomplish tasks with ease. But when you don't feel so enthusiastic, the second success cycle, discipline, must kick in. During those times when you don't "feel like" doing the tasks you must to create success, call on discipline. Decide how many "efforts" you will accomplish that day. When you can discipline yourself to make some form of effort, even if it's small efforts toward the process — your enthusiasm begins to rekindle. The cycle continues. Be a person of discipline. This amazing discipline breeds results and results breed enthusiasm. It is a continuous cycle . . . "The Success Cycle."

What small steps are you willing to take even when burnout is resting on your heavy shoulders? Rely on your discipline to take you through the fire. You'll be amazed at the way your enthusiasm begins to rekindle. You will be just a few short steps from reveling in your enthusiasm for personal growth and mastery once again . . . until the next time!

When you first try using "The Success Cycle" you may need to take it slow. You may need "Success Cycle Training Wheels." But once you've tried it a few times, you can remove the training wheels, and ride the Success Cycle in a continuous loop without even thinking.

All great leaders have conviction and the ability to convey that conviction in a way that empowers the people they lead.

I trust you will continue this journey of great leadership, and you will understand the power of human behavior, break through negative belief barriers and cultivate your conviction. Through your conviction you will create a significant legacy in the people you lead.

ABOUT
LISA JIMENEZ, M.ED.

*E*mpower your people to break through procrastination and shatter *self-limiting beliefs with programs and resources from Lisa Jimenez,* *M.Ed. Lisa helps people overcome fear and fight through the obstacles that* *choke their potential. Her book,* Stop Procrastination! Ending Self-Sabotage to Achieve What You Really Want, *has helped thousands of* *people reach higher levels of success. She can help you, too. Lisa teaches* *from her "real world" experience of developing a large business while* *raising three children. She received her Masters Degree in Educational* *Leadership from Florida Atlantic University. Call now for rates and avail-*ability and to request your free copy of Breakthroughs, *an annual catalog* *full of items and ideas that improve business and life strategies.*

Contact information:
G.C.P. Communications
4691 N. University Drive, Suite 449
Coral Springs, FL 33067
℃ (800) 489-7391
℃ (954) 755-3670
fax (954) 796-0549
e-mail: Lisajmenez@aol.com

A Simple
Leadership Secret

By Rick Segel, CSP

What is leadership? That question has been debated for centuries. Why do some men and woman have the ability to lead other men and women? It isn't just leadership — it is the art or skill of great leadership. It is leadership from which legends are made. It is the type of leadership that converts casual observers into fanatic followers. It's about the type of leader you want to follow: the type of leader in whom you put your trust and faith because they make you believe in yourself first. Then they make you believe and respect them.

What do great leaders do? What can we learn from them? The strange thing about those questions is that when you see great leaders, they don't look or act the way you might expect. They don't necessarily have that swagger of a General George S. Patton or the aura of an Adolph Hitler. Let's set politics aside; of course Hitler was one of the most despicable characters in history, but the man could lead. Anyone who can lead a people to do what he had them do has to be acknowledged.

Many times, great leaders are the man or woman next door. They are average, everyday people who do the right things over and over again. And even when they make a mistake, we forgive them and still follow. Why? What is that magic formula that business executives have chased as if it were the holy grail? Executives have long realized that good leadership converts easily into good management, and good management converts into bottom line results. Good leadership is bankable.

Great leaders generally succeed in any endeavor they undertake. We follow the winners, we jump on their bandwagons, and we invest in companies that hire the leaders with the right stuff. Do we seek heroes? Absolutely. A hero or great leader excites us while relaxing us at the exact same time. It is a feeling of security just knowing that a real leader is in charge. We don't worry — it's exciting because great leadership is a combination of vision, creativity and detail. They see the big picture but completely understand the importance of the tiniest detail.

Great leaders understand the power of one — the power and diference one person can make. They understand their own significance but are not controlled by it. They understand that the power of one might just be coming from the lowliest frontline person. That is what I call mutual respect. Without respect there is no leader, but it must be mutual. Too many times people mistake fear-inspiring behavior for leadership. It is time for us to realize that using fear to motivate is only a short-term remedy.

Fear only inhibits people. No one wants to try anything different because the fear of failure will result in negative influences. (That's a nice way of saying that you get yelled at or screamed at.) What really is happening is that we are discounting our people. We are not giving them full value when we try to motivate someone by saying things like, "I can't believe how stupid you are!" People get overly cautious and will resist change. Why? Because change represents doing something different and the emotional response will be fear.

This is the very essence of real leadership although I am approaching it backwards: backwards because what I am saying is to look at the negative results and reverse them to find the positive. Instead of the negative stimuli, try the positive stimuli. Instead of looking for the bad, look for the good and build on that. Michael LeBoeuf, the great speaker and writer, says, "The behavior that is rewarded is the behavior that is repeated." Think about the last time someone put you down. What was your first reaction? Probably it was to discredit that person. Did you ever have anyone come up to you and say things like, "You look tired!" and you're not? Or say, "You gained weight!" or "How much weight did you gain?"

Don't you feel like replying, "Who are you to tell me that, Mr. Lovehandles?" Do we want to follow this person? No way. Now reverse it to the feeling that you have when someone tells you that you look radiant or healthy or slim. How do you feel? Wonderful; you have an extra spring in your step. You feel exhilarated. Don't we wear certain clothes because every time we wear them we get compliments and that makes us feel good? Is there any better feeling in the world after you lose weight and everyone is complimenting you? Let's take it another step. Can't we all remember the time when we had a boss who pulled us aside and said, "Nice job" or "I like the work you're doing"? How did it make you feel? What did you think of your boss?

Are we straying too far from the point? We are talking about leadership and I'm talking about compliments. That's right, compliments, because I believe that finding the good in people is probably one of the largest building blocks to great leadership. When was the last time you saw the Academy Awards, or any award ceremony for that matter, when someone came to the podium and said, "I want to thank the person who put me down." NEVER. Winners always thank the person who believed in them.

Leadership is a personal thing. We judge our leaders, and for that matter the issues of the world, according to how they affect us. Great leaders touch us personally. Tip O'Neill, the former Speaker of the House of Representatives in Washington, used to say, "All politics are local." People don't look at the big picture — they look at the way things affect them personally. So if all politics is local, all leadership is personal!

Now I have really opened up the proverbial "can of worms." Some of you are probably thinking, is he nuts? Just give everybody a compliment, and you'll be a great leader. I don't think so. There are compliments and there are those back slapping, eye winking, you look great, transparent gestures that are as fake as the person wearing a $500.00 suit and driving a new Mercedes Benz whose credit cards are maxed out and who is three months behind in car lease payments. I am NOT talking about that. I am talking about the power of compliments, which, when done effectively, can change lives and become the foundation for leadership. Let me share my experiences that have made me a true believer.

My first exposure to the concept was when I was running my family's women's clothing store. I employed thirty-six women, almost all of them over forty with the majority over fifty. They all worked part-time, and very few worked for just the money. Most enjoyed the social aspects of working and being active, productive people. The most difficult part about managing and leading this group was simply that their first priority was not to the job and that very few were motivated by money. The issue was self-worth. Many of these women were widows or were living with husbands from another era — the era of male dominance and a world that revolved around the man. I was young and thrown into the women's apparel and the retail business. But I was smart enough to know what I didn't know. I was never afraid to ask questions. "How would you do this?" or "How should I do that?" "What do you think about that situation?" I asked questions and I thanked them. It sounds simple enough, and I certainly didn't think I was doing something special.

Friends of mine would stop in the store from time to time and always tell me how they didn't envy me having to manage these types of employees. I would just laugh it off and think little of it. When I would visit their companies, I would see that they employed or worked with people more their own age. But every time I would visit one of their companies, there were always new people there. People would be coming and going. At first I thought I was lucky to employ older workers who didn't change jobs quite so often. But as my business grew, I started to hire younger workers, and they stayed just as the older people did. The joke around the store was that the only way you could leave was if you died.

People started to ask me what was my secret in managing people, and I would always respond the same way. Ask people their opinions, try to use them if you can, and if you can't, still thank them and explain to all why you did or didn't use their opinion. Twenty-five years later I finally realized what I had done. All I did was compliment them. By asking their opinion, I was respecting them as human beings and making them feel good about themselves. I was boosting their self-esteem. I had them believe in themselves first, and then anything I ever asked of them was never a problem.

The strength of the concept is simple. Make sure you are always asking or touching as many people as possible. It's the same as speaking in public. When I speak from the platform, I make eye contact with every member of the audience. It lets people know you care about them. My future daughter-in-law recently told me about one of those unwritten "rules of etiquette." She explained to me that at every party you should speak to everyone at least twice. Not a bad rule to live by.

As I got older and wiser, or so I thought, I lost that leadership edge by playing favorites, listening to some but not others, or just totally forgetting to do those basics. I had been there and done that, and I didn't need opinions. People started to leave the store and people's blind faith in me started to wane. Yet, I still didn't realize what I had done or not done.

The next experience I had with this secret weapon of leadership was when I was involved in chapter leadership of the New England Speakers Association. I had just been elected to the board of directors, which was a very prestigious and highly competitive position for this 190-person group of professional speakers. Speakers have no shortage of egos, so leadership positions are much sought after and highly respected among the group. Every month we had a meeting, and every month we would have what is called "spotlight speakers." These were usually new speakers who would address the group for 7 to 10 minutes. This was always a big day in the life of a new speaker. There would be hours of preparation for those few short minutes. At the end of the speech, the rest of the group would write an evaluation of their performance. Somehow I thought that it was a cold practice. So when I heard someone who had real talent, I would go home that night and send a letter explaining how I felt and encouraging that speaker as much as I could. I didn't do anything for the ones I didn't like.

I never realized the power of what I was doing. I started to bond with these people in ways I never thought possible. They would mention that act as a turning point in their lives. I forged relationships I never believed would be possible. Maybe my being on the board of directors added a level of prestige, or maybe it was just me, but whatever it was, it formed a strong base of followers that helped me eventually become president of the organization with unquestioned support. All I was doing was giving a compliment, but it meant so much more.

In all of my speeches, I talk about the power of compliments, although the word sounds so shallow considering the awesome power it holds. Every time I speak, I wear a Tabasco necktie — the kind that has the logo of the company boldly printed across the tie. Tacky would be the best description of the tie. But every time I wear that tie, I always get a compliment. My response is pretty routine now. I will say something like, "I wanted to wear something hot if I was going to be in _____." Then I would then name the city I was in or I would say, "Because you mentioned that, I will include it in my speech."

When I would get to the section about compliments, I would tell the audience that I had done a survey before we began that proves the power. I would ask the audience how many people complimented my tie and me. There are always at least seven or eight people. I thank them and tell them how wonderful they made me feel. I tell them that I am not a very good-looking man and very rarely receive compliments but "You people made me feel as if I were king of the world. Just because of a compliment." Then I proceed to tell them a true story that happened to me a few years ago.

I was speaking in Connecticut and I was all done. I had a two- and-a-half-hour ride ahead of me and was eager to get home. Just as I started to leave, the meeting planner came rushing up to me all excited and proceeded to tell me about a fashion show they were going to have after lunch. She said, "You come from the fashion industry. You will love it." Having spent twenty-five years in the fashion business, my feeling was that if I never go to another fashion show as long as I live, I will be a happy camper. But I was obligated. So I sat at the round lunch table and made small talk. Then the shop owner who was going to moderate the show appeared. He had a full head of hair; I was jealous. He was wearing a double-breasted Italian wool suit with a white T-shirt. He had a real attitude of superiority. He must have had ten gold chains around his neck. I thought he was wearing a Mr. T starter set. He spoke out of the side of his mouth as if he were a cross between Vic Damone and Frank Sinatra, and trying to say, "I am cool and you are nothing!" Then he made a statement which really put me into orbit. He said, "The next exclusive collection from the exclusive collection of" and then named his store. I had the same merchandise in my retail store. What was so exclusive about it?

I hated him. I hated his attitude. I hated his demeanor. I hated the words he was saying. As far as I was concerned, there was nothing good about this man. Yet, as the fashion show came to a close, I said to myself that I should go up to him and tell him he did a good job. We both came from the same industry and I should be a pro. I didn't want to. I stood there, arguing with myself for a few brief seconds that seemed like an eternity. Go ahead. I don't want to. Go ahead. I felt like I had Jiminy Cricket on my shoulder.

I finally mustered enough courage to approach the obnoxious soul. I introduced myself, and before I had a chance to give my cursory congratulations, he said, "I know who you are. I've read some of your articles and I have one of your tape series." He continued, "It's really good." I thanked him, but I just wanted to acknowledge him and get out of there as fast as I could — remember, I couldn't stand him. When I said, " You did a nice job on the fashion show," his voice changed, almost breaking up with emotion, and he uttered, "Do you really think so?" I said, "Yes," not really meaning it fully. Then he said the following words fighting back the tears, " To get a compliment like that from YOU. I will never forget this moment as long as I live." I liked that man! If someone that obnoxious can make me melt that quickly with a compliment, what could a compliment do to the people you encounter?

I have told that story more than a hundred times and I receive letters and calls from people in my audiences telling me how that simple tool has affected their lives. Are we just winning friends and influencing people? Is this merely a tool from Dale Carnegie? No, I believe it is far more powerful then we even realize. It is truly one of the solid foundations of leadership. It is believing in people, empowerment if you will. But it all starts with the simple seed of saying something nice about someone. I'm sure better men or women than I can define the phenomenon better or perhaps even in more technical terms, but whatever it is, it WORKS. Try it and watch what happens. Leadership will seek you out. People will start to believe in you because you made them believe in themselves.

ABOUT
RICK SEGEL, CSP

Rick Segel, CSP, helps organizations and businesses sell and market more effectively, with an imaginative, creative and humorous flair. His 25 years of retail experience can be applied to all types and sizes of companies. Rick's speaking topics include customer service, selling, marketing and leadership skills. He is consistently one of the highest-rated speakers at any of the conferences at which he presents (and has been awarded the Certified Speaking Professional designation by the National Speakers Association).

Rick has been a featured speaker in 39 states and Canada and has delivered over 750 presentations. He has spoken at over 90 malls, trade shows, corporations and associations. Rick has authored five audio programs and a training video program entitled, "Stop Losing Sales." He represented the retail community on a Sally Jesse Raphael Show entitled, "Buy It, Wear It and Return It." His laugh and learn style make him a crowd pleaser wherever he goes.

Contact information:
Rick Segel & Associates
One Wheatland Street
Burlington, MA 01803
℃ (781) 272-9995
fax (781) 272-9996
e-mail: rsegel@aol.com
www.ricksegel.com

MENTOR LEADERSHIP — REPLICATING YOUR PERSONAL BEST IN OTHERS

"Management problems always turn out to be people problems."
— John Peet

By Mike Monahan

Successful organizations in today's times are those organizations that have a focus on the needs of customers, are responsive to the market forces, understand their competition, are adaptable to change, and use leadership to build effective relationships with their employees.

Business literature is filled with references to what makes a good leader. Most contain lists of traits or characteristics of good leaders. I believe what a leader is is a reflection of what a leader does. Successful leaders are people who understand why people work and what makes them want to do well and act accordingly. Good leaders use leverage tools, such as the following:

They build an effective work force by

Hiring good people — This sounds simple, yet most leaders find it incredibly difficult. Get personally involved in the process. Make certain that the job descriptions used by your company's human resources department to advertise and screen candidates are based on the actual competencies needed for the job. Involve your front-line staff in the interviewing and hiring process. If faced with choosing between skill and attitude, go with attitude. All other things being equal, a willing worker will learn and add to the overall spirit of cooperation desired. Look specifically for the following traits in new-hire candidates:

- A strong performance ethic
- A cooperative, not a competitive, mindset
- A high level of communication skills
- An expressed desire to get along with others
- Appreciation of complementary skills of fellow staff members

Soliciting active senior management support — Keep your boss and your boss's boss informed of what you are doing to meet the needs of the organization. Invite them to lunch with your staff. Prepare "performance testimonials" — letters, notes and transcribed phone messages showing the results of your efforts. Be generous in the mention of individuals and teams responsible for getting things done.

Giving extra effort to problems that matter immediately to the organization — Your organization's crises are your crises!

Being competitive in obtaining adequate budget and resources — There will always be some rationing of resources in today's organizations. You have a responsibility to know what a "fair share" is and pro-actively seek it. Don't look at budgeting as a once-a-year unpleasant task but as a management tool that will allow you to accomplish your purpose.

Creating organizational systems that are compatible to working in teams — Teams provide consistency, creativity and a working environment conducive to productivity. Understanding the dynamics of teams and ensuring rewards and incentives promotes teamwork.

Providing the necessary training for your staff — Although poor performance is often blamed on lack of motivation, study after study reveals that more often people don't know how to do something. Training not only increases abilities but is also a visible sign of management interest in the individual and promotes a willingness to increase performance.

They create a positive work environment by

Making feedback, recognition, and reward part of regular staff meeting agendas — Remember: recognized and rewarded results are repeated!

Becoming mutually accountable for results — Make yourself answer to your staff for your role and responsibilities. A simple tool to do this is to ask your staff daily:

- What worked well today?
- What made you feel good about working here today?
- What are you proud of today?
- Who deserves special recognition today?
- What didn't work today?
- What caused problems today?
- What made you angry today?
- What took too long, or was too complicated?
- Are there any things that we did that took too many people, or took too many actions?
- What did we have to do that didn't contribute to our purpose?
- What sorts of extraneous things did we attempt to do today?

You will be surprised how often, at the end of the day, people feel pretty exhausted but aren't really sure what they've accomplished. Asking these questions indicates your desire to communicate and that you are interested in them. You create feedback opportunities for reassuring your staff and creating your own improvement expectations. Questions like "What are you proud of today?" measure what they have done and set the stage for people to take actions to be able to answer that question in the positive the next time you ask it. The question "Who deserves special recognition for his or her accomplishments today?" helps you find those people who deserve special recognition.

Celebrating team accomplishments — Public acknowledgment of group or team accomplishments is crucial to reinforcing the successes. The key word here is celebrate. Have some fun, make it public — and do it often!

Creating an understanding and measuring the acceptance of a purpose and common goals — Assuming that people truly know what and why we are doing the things we do is dangerous. Each individual must know his or her role in the bigger picture and how that role is a part of an overall whole. To the extent that you can create common and shared goals, you can enhance both commitment and desire to perform in your staff. Have discussions with your staff about the "why" of each functional area in your organization. Have discussions about their roles in keeping your organization viable in today's marketplace.

Promoting clear rules of behavior/communication procedures in your area of influence — Your staff should be able to answer the following questions:

- Whose work do I affect?
- Whose work will change as a result of changing my work?

Consider changes in work procedures, materials used, regulations that have to be followed, people who must be involved, for example.

- Whom do I need to seek out to do a better job?
- Who has experience with my task who could help me perform my work?
- Whose advice should I seek?
- What company knowledge can I use to achieve excellence?
- Whom should I keep informed about what I'm doing?
- Whom should I tell about my work — at its inception, during its creation and at its completion?
- When do I need to just do what I'm told?
- When should I ask what to do?
- When should I act independently?
- Whom am I serving?
- Who is my customer, and what does my customer want?
- What external stakeholders must be satisfied with my work?
- What does my work impact in the larger organization?
- How should I get along with others?
- Who else uses the same resources I need?

- How can we make decisions about the most effective use of those resources?
- How does my work schedule affect the schedules of others?
- What is considered good productivity?
- How do we deal with conflict?
- How do we solve problems?

They drive change.

Don't wait for change to occur — there is plenty that needs to be done that too often falls in the category of "too hard" because of the fear of change. It is generally much easier to take a pro-active stance and make changes now rather than later responding to a change imposed from above.

They get results.

Nothing speaks like results. An organization that maximizes revenue, controls expenses, builds positive relationships and truly practices excellent customer service will develop a reputation for results that will benefit you in many ways.

They are knowledgeable.

Be competent — How many times have you said something about someone in a leadership position related to how little they know? You don't have to know every technical detail of your staff's work, but you must know what is going on and who needs help — as well as every aspect of your job.

Balance your demands for your staff's productivity with a respect for your staff's production capability. Stephen Covey refers to this as the Production/Production Capability (P/PC) continuum and insists that when we drive people too hard, we actually diminish their capability to perform. Training, time-off, rewards and personal recognition all contribute to enhancing the production capability in our staff. (Covey, 1989)

Be decisive — Leaders who can't make decisions lose others' respect and subsequently lose their influence over others. Collect your data, review your options and worry about being right — but make the decision.

Don't inspire others to oppose you — Some people will not like you just because of your title. Some people won't like you because of decisions you make that influence their lives. Most people will make their decisions about you based on their perception of how they are treated by you. Respect, fairness and just plain pleasantness will go a long way towards building relationships that support your leadership role.

Expect the best from others — People tend to respond to the expectations that are set for them.

Understand people — not everyone is like you. Make it your business to know how people are motivated, what they like and dislike, what encourages desired behaviors, and what their expectations of you are.

Create an environment in which failure is not fatal — Don't accept sloppy, incomplete or poor quality work. Rather, do encourage your staff to try new procedures, attempt novel solutions to old problems and creatively seek process improvements. The only way to get the focused effort of your staff is to allow failure when a good-faith effort has been made.

Encourage others — even if they are only close — Perfection may be an infrequent event. When people are working hard and getting close, provide the encouragement and support needed to help them stay engaged and trying.

Model successful behavior — Perhaps no other leadership trait is as important as modeling. You are a role model for your staff. Everyone watches to see what you do and how you do it. Positive actions, ethical behavior, commitment to productivity and adherence to the behavioral norms of your organization will breed similar behaviors in most of your staff.

Keep your own motivation high — Casey Stengel, the longtime manager of the New York Yankees reportedly once said, "The toughest part of management was keeping the two or three people who liked me away from the rest of the team who hated me!" We tend to be disproportionately affected by the few malcontents, sociopaths and whiners on our staff. Stay focused on the positive contributions of your staff, care for your own production capability, build a support network among other managers in your organization, seek a mentor, and stay in the game.

The Mentor Leader

Throughout history, great things have been accomplished by ordinary people influenced by extraordinary people — leaders. Textbooks and cultural lore are filled with the leadership accomplishments of the likes of Moses, Sir Francis Drake, George Washington and Abraham Lincoln. In my own life, I have been influenced by great contemporary leaders, such as John F. Kennedy, Martin Luther King Jr. and General Colin Powell. I have also been personally influenced by leaders whose accomplishments affected my personal and professional life. Some of the most powerful influence has come from those leaders who took a personal interest in me and provided me with a mentoring relationship. Their willingness to share their wisdom and coach me to greater performance has had a significant positive impact on my personal success. Three of these leaders are models for the mentor leader I am describing in this chapter.

As a young Navy enlistee, my life was forever altered by a naval officer named Greg Gregory. Greg proved to me and to my fellow Navy men that one person can make a difference in the lives of many. Greg was a leader who modeled integrity, compassion and an unwavering belief in our ability to be as good as he expected. Greg also took an interest in each of us personally and provided direct help in planning for our individual successes. As my mentor, Greg helped me navigate the bureaucracy of the organization and gain important promotions.

Midway through my first career I had the opportunity to work for and benefit from the wisdom and absolute commitment to excellence embodied by Captain Dolores Cornelius. Dolores was a leader ahead of her time. Dolores consistently demonstrated an equal interest in both the achievement and growth of her staff. Her work ethic and her attention to accomplishment with style are lessons that serve me well today. As my mentor, Dolores helped me develop high-impact leadership skills such as performance coaching and dealing with seniors in the organization.

Ten years ago I was managing a training program that was buffeted by political maneuvering at higher levels and had been poorly led by a senior executive who was subsequently fired. Our new boss was an energetic and outgoing man named Mel Hamm. Mel walked into our lives and began a process of restoring credibility to our organization and making us all feel good about what we were accomplishing. He was willing to stand up to the outside naysayers and helped us create a work place that was ultimately praised by all and served as a model for future organizations. Mel's knowledge and ability to work with a wide variety of people in such a positive manner serve me well today. As my mentor, Mel helped me learn to deal with adversity, think strategically and build a cooperative workforce.

Greg Gregory, Dolores Cornelius and Mel Hamm all had a similar characteristic: They were extremely desirous of helping those who were interested in learning how to be as successful as they were. They recreated themselves while helping others. This is a form of mentoring that is one of the most important roles of a leader. A 1997 study by the Center for Creative Leadership concluded that formal developmental relationships, such as coaching and mentoring, are the most effective ways to promote the growth and development of leaders in an organization. The vast majority of CEO's report having had mentors as a key success factor in their careers. (Survey in *Chief Executive*, 1994)

The traditional image of a mentor is an interesting one. People usually perceive mentors as someone older, in the same business and of the same gender and race. The mentor is the embodiment of who you want to be. The word mentor comes from the name of a man who was asked by Odysseus to serve as a teacher for his son. In the traditional context, a mentor was seen as a teacher, or someone to help another advance professionally. Through the years, mentoring has evolved into something greater and much more powerful. Mentor leadership is a powerful tool for both personal and organizational development. Some of the things mentor leadership can do are:

Advance the personal and career development of people. There are no specifically designed roles for mentors, no mentor degrees, certifications or manuals. Thus, the roles may change radically from person to person. Sometimes mentors perform the roles of inquisitor, examiner, and reality-tester — at other times, teacher, counselor and friend. Some mentors assume all of these roles, others only one or two. Additionally, these varying roles are assumed to enhance both the personal and professional life of the protégé, not only the career-development side.

Many people may be mentors, each providing us with a piece of what we need for success. Different mentors can provide different gifts. For example, you might have a mentor to help you in your profession, another who stimulates your creativity, another who can teach you to be a better listener and another who shows you how to be a better volunteer. Mentors can tap different facets of our lives, developing us in many ways.

Mentoring gives us an opportunity to give back. One curious thing about mentorhood that is not readily apparent — but that one discovers after participation — is that learning flows both ways. The mentor learns from the protégé, just as the protégé learns from the mentor. The growth process is reciprocal. That is the magic of mentorhood.

A mentor can be anyone offering the help one needs. Age does not necessarily carry with it inherent wisdom. We can have mentors younger than we are from whom we can learn a great deal. We can also have peers as mentors. When we make an assumption that we can only learn from someone older, we deprive ourselves of many learning opportunities and fulfilling relationships.

Also mentors can be a different gender and race from the protégé. The purpose of mentorhood is to learn. If we limit our mentors and protégés to members of the same gender and race, then we limit the potential for growth. Diverse perspectives on life enable us to see the world in a different way, thus stimulating the mind and cultivating the intellect. We should seek mentors and protégés who are different from ourselves, challenging us to nudge our minds and discover new worlds.

Mentor relationships must be sought pro-actively. While many believe that having the right mentor is a matter of being at the right place at the right time, establishing a mentor/protégé relationship can be strategic as well. The key to selecting a good mentor is first to identify what (not who) you need. Thinking about your career needs and the kind of help you require will enable you to seek and select a mentor whose talents and experiences will be beneficial to you. Do not be afraid to actively seek a mentor, for the riches you gain will far outweigh any uncomfortable feelings associated with asking.

Being able to share knowledge and wisdom with others makes one a good mentor. Prestigious and successful individuals can certainly be good mentors, providing good advice on career goals, increasing visibility and offering encouragement and enhancing growth opportunities; however, individual differences, such as leadership style, work ethic and mentor expectations, may impede your growth. Good mentors are people who, regardless of their titles, will challenge a protégé in accordance with his or her needs, readiness and aspirations.

A mentor relationship focuses on accomplishing growth objectives, not on fulfilling a time commitment. Before you begin a relationship with a mentor or protégé, decide what you want to accomplish. As the skills, attitudes and confidence of the protégé change, the mentor should pull back and let the protégé go his or her own way. The goal in a mentor-protégé relationship is to move beyond the restricting confines of dependency to the higher state of interdependency. Although a mentor and protégé may maintain contact for a long time, the relationship can have time parameters.

Mentorhood is not a complicated process. As a mentor leader, you may simply just give pointers for improvement at strategic leverage points in your staff's daily work or create opportunities for your staff to succeed.

Mentor-protégé expectations are different for everyone. Individuals of all kinds seek mentors for many of the same reasons: resources, visibility, enhanced skills or counsel; however, each individual or protégé brings different expectations. Successful mentors assess where a protégé is, not where the protégé should be. The mentor provides ample opportunity for "expectation discussions" to take place, which in turn will guide and enrich the experience.

The key to successful mentorhood is commitment to the growth and development of another individual. A mentor helps people develop their skills, abilities and understanding in the following areas:

- Understanding the organization's culture, mission and goals
- The rationale behind policies and procedures
- How to improve productivity
- Opportunities for job advancement and promotion
- The effect of external events on their job
- How their organization compares to others
- What is happening in other areas of the company
- Where the organization stands on local, regional and national issues
- How to build important relationships
- How to deal with work-life issues
- How to deal with conflict
- Key success indicators valued by senior executives

Specifically, mentor leaders serve in the following roles:

Communicator
- Encourages two-way exchange of information
- Listens to protégé's career concerns and responds appropriately
- Establishes an environment for open interaction
- Schedules uninterrupted time to meet with protégé

Counselor
- Works with protégé to identify and understand career-related skills, interest, and values

- Helps protégé evaluate appropriateness of career options
- Helps protégé think through work-life balance implications of current and considered career choices

Coach

- Helps to clarify performance goals and plan strategies to achieve them
- Teaches managerial and technical training
- Reinforces effective on-the-job performance
- Recommends specific behaviors in which the protégé needs improvement
- Clarifies and communicates organizational goals and objectives
- Serves as a role model to demonstrate successful professional behaviors

Broker

- Expands the protégé's network of professional contacts
- Helps bring together different protégés who might mutually benefit by helping each other
- Helps link protégés with appropriate educational or employment opportunities
- Helps the protégé identify resources required for career progression

Advocate

- Intervenes on the protégé's behalf, representing the protégé's concerns to higher-level management for redress on specific issues
- Arranges for the protégé to participate in high-visibility activities within or outside the organization

Advisor

- Communicates the informal and formal realities of progression in the organization
- Recommends training opportunities from which the protégé could benefit

- Recommends appropriate strategies for career direction
- Reviews the protégé's development plan on a regular basis
- Helps the protégé identify obstacles to career progression and to take appropriate action

Personal-Best Mentor Leadership Experience

With regard to mentor leadership, experience is the best teacher. Most leaders learn what to do by trying it themselves or by watching others. The problem is that not all of what is done or observed is ideal or even appropriate. Therefore, it is important to base your mentor leadership practices on the best of what you do or see done by those you respect. Such examples provide role models for effective mentor leadership. (Adapted from Kouzes and Posner *The Leadership Challenge*)

Instructions: Take about ten minutes to write some notes about your best mentor experience.

Recall a time when, in your opinion, you or someone else did the very best as a mentor-leader for another person or people. Your mentor-leadership experience can be with your present job, with a previous employer or in your personal life. It can be in the public or private sector, as an appointed, selected, or "emerged" leader, for pay or as a volunteer. Choose one that you believe is your best or the best you've seen. Write a brief description of that experience.

_____

_____

_____

_____

Think about the choice you just made, and use the space provided to summarize five to seven things that you or someone else did as a mentor-leader. Consider what caused this leadership experience to be your personal best mentor/mentoring experience.

1. _____

2. _____

3. _____

4. _____

5. _____

6. _____

7. _____

What words best describe the character (the quality, nature, personality, tone, special mood, etc.) of this experience?

_____

_____

_____

_____

What would you say were the major lessons or morals about mentor leadership that you learned from this experience?

_____

_____

_____

What were the results of the mentoring experience for you or others? What was learned? What was accomplished?

_____

_____

_____

_____

Action Plan for Becoming a More Effective Mentor Leader

What mentor practice or behavior do you want to improve?

_____

_____

List the specifics of what you would like to be better able to do.

_____

_____

What specific actions could you take? What options do you have?

_____

_____

What actions will you take to meet your improvement goal?

_____

_____

What is the first action you will take to improve your mentor-leadership ability? Who will be involved? When will you begin? Include action, people involved and target date.

_____

_____

Complete this sentence: "I will know I have improved my mentor leadership skills when . . . ."

_____

_____

On what date do you plan to review your progress?

The Ten Commitments of Mentor Leadership

1. Search for challenging opportunities to help others change, grow, innovate and improve.

2. Help others to experiment, take risks and learn from the accompanying mistakes.

3. Create an uplifting and ennobling future for your mentees.

4. Build a common purpose.

5. Foster collaboration by promoting cooperative goals and building trust.

6. Strengthen others by sharing power and information.

7. Set an example for others by behaving in ways that are consistent with your stated values.

8. Plan small wins that promote consistent progress and build commitment to agreed upon actions.

9. Recognize all who contribute to the success of the mentoring.

10. Celebrate accomplishments regularly.

Replicating the best you do in others is the highest calling of leadership. You have the ability as a mentor-leader to bring the best to your organization and the people you are responsible for developing.

References:

Biebowitz, Z. and Schlossberg, N. "Training Managers for their Role in a Career Development System." *Training and Development Journal*, July 1981.

Bridges, W. *Managing Transitions: Making the Most of Change*. *Reading*, MA: Addison-Wesley, 1991.

Covey, S. *The Seven Habits of Highly Effective People*. New York: Simon and Schuster, 1989.

Gubman, E. *The Talent Solution: Aligning Strategy and People to Achieve Extraordinary Results*. New York: McGraw Hill, 1998.

Kouzes, J. and Posner, B. *The Leadership Challenge*. San Francisco: Jossey-Bass, 1995.

Monahan, M., et al. *Where There's Change There's Opportunity*. Roswell, GA: James and Brookfield, 1998.

Noer, D. Breaking Free: *A Prescription for Personal and Organization Change*. San Francisco: Jossey-Bass, 1996.

ABOUT
MIKE MONAHAN

*M*ike Monahan is the Managing Partner for M2 Learning Resources, *a human performance improvement consulting and training practice. Mike has worked as a clinician, manager and executive in several organizational settings. He has developed a particular interest in the needs of transforming organizations, focusing on helping teams and individuals improve performance and tend to the human side of change. Mike conducts leader and manager competency development sessions and has a series of customizable training interventions for all levels of supervisors and managers. Mike is co-author of the acclaimed book* Where There's Change, There's Opportunity! *and has numerous articles published in professional journals. Mike is a frequent speaker at national conferences and has consulting clients ranging from small business practices to Fortune 500 companies.*

Contact information:
M2 Learning Resources
1153 Bergen Parkway, Suite M-181
Evergreen, CO 80439
℃ (800) 759-2881
fax (303) 674-3186
e-mail: M2HRA@aol.com

Get Good, Get Great, Get Going! Steps To Success After Setback

by Connie Payton

Believe it or not, leaders are not immune from failure. What? A leader failing? Suffering setback? Say it isn't so! Sometimes it is difficult for us to associate a leader with failure. My idea of a leader or a real winner is someone at the very top of his game: confident, energetic and with a bright smile and dress-for-success appearance. On the other hand, my idea of a failure is someone who's slow to respond and depressed, with a negative attitude and shabby appearance. Perhaps, I am guilty of stereotyping two extreme types of people, but give me a winner any day.

Some of the most successful people we know today were at one time or another defeated. For example, Michael Jordan did not make the basketball team as a high school sophomore. Can you imagine that? The greatest basketball player we will ever see in our lifetime "slam-dunked!" I wonder: where is that coach now? Actually, he probably did Michael a big favor. Not being chosen certainly got Michael's attention. When he could not find his name on the list of players who did make the team, he went home and cried. Then, the real winner came out of him: He renewed his focus and continued to practice with determination. I, and a lot of other fans are so glad Michael Jordan did not give up. In fact, as I was writing this chapter, my seven-year-old son, Jonathan, looked over my shoulders and saw Michael Jordan's name and immediately said, "No mommy, Michael Jordan did not fail; he retired!" His expression was "Let's get that straight!"

I have always considered myself a winner and a leader. I had my share of successes in high school and college. I am certainly not one to back down from a challenge. In fact, I have a friend who accuses me of loving life on the razor's edge. I am a firm believer that hard work and determination are the keys to success. Until the spring of 1992, I never really doubted my leadership abilities. I worked with IBM for more than fifteen years in various marketing and technical positions. Full employment was an IBM tradition and most of us had a "cradle-to-grave" mentality. I had always prepared myself for worst-case-scenarios, but even I was surprised that fateful day when my manager called me into his office to tell me about the new ranking scale that IBM was going to start using in addition to the usual performance evaluation. This new method would rank all employees in the same department, regardless of their level or job classification. Employees would be ranked from the highest to the lowest. The highest ranked employees would be in the top percentile, then there would be the middle percentile, and finally the bottom. The whole process was a way of eliminating the bottom ten per cent. The catch was our performance evaluation had nothing to do with our ranking. We would be ranked by the entire management team. Even managers within the department who did not know us or our accomplishments could rank us against an employee who reported to him. To me, this process reeked of favoritism, especially when my manager told me that I was ranked at the "top of the bottom 10%." I was amazed, especially since I was a "two" performer on a five-point scale. I knew then that it was time for me to take action.

When my manager finished his presentation, I looked him straight in the eyes and calmly said, "I am not at the bottom of anything. I was raised in one of the worst housing projects in New Orleans. I survived.

I not only survived, I have thrived while none of my male peers made it out. After what I have lived through, to willingly accept being ranked at the bottom of anything would negate my accomplishments. It is time for me to make some changes."

My manager, to his credit, tried to talk me out of it. He said, "Connie, don't take this personally; this is just a process."

I said "I understand, but I have been at the bottom before; I refuse to go backwards." With that, I, along with thousands of other brave souls, willingly or otherwise left the safety of IBM to face a world that was not so eager to accept us.

Despite my anger, it was exciting to start over. I decided that this was a great opportunity to try something different. After extensive research and interviews, I got the bright idea to start my own residential and commercial cleaning business. Armed with what I thought was a perfect marketing and business plan, I mapped out my territory and went to work. The easy part was selling my services. The tough part was finding good help that showed up consistently.

Eventually, after several years of struggling to keep things going, I ran out of money. Then I had to face the grim reality that I had failed. With no money to fall back on, I became a cleaning lady simply to survive.

Before long my confidence faded. My downward spiral was swift and overwhelming. I had gone through a lot in a short period of time: One day I was a professional with a great job and security, and in the blink of an eye, I became a cleaning lady. Things would get worse before they would get better. The hard physical work took its toll. I was tired all of the time, my resistance was low and I was constantly getting sick. I was working day and night just to keep my head above water. My days and nights were a blur. Finally, I had to admit to myself that I was not getting anywhere. I was too ashamed to admit my defeat to anyone else. I hoped if I did not say anything, it would just go away. Then one day, while working alone in a customer's house, I heard a voice say to me:

"Connie Payton . . . cleaning is not your final destination!" I knew that I was hearing the voice of God. I stopped vacuuming and looked up toward the Heavens and said "Don't Clown, God; you know that we don't have any more money!" After hearing that voice, I felt a sense of relief. Then I started to question myself. The more questions I asked, the more I needed to ask. Slowly, I began to feel a glimmer of hope. I knew I had to find a way to make a comeback.

Whenever we suffer setbacks or life-changing experiences, we need to take time to regroup. This a period of transition, which is not a good time to make any major decision or hasty move. Taking time to reflect allows a person to see things a whole lot clearer. Initially, I used this period to feel sorry for myself. Then I realized that a pity party was a waste of time, so, I got over my hurt feelings and made up my mind to move forwards, not backwards. Often, when we suffer a major setback, we waste valuable time wallowing in self-pity and looking backwards. Instead of looking backwards, we should look at a setback as a learning experience. Without a doubt, some very good lessons came out of all the tumultuous changes and upheaval I experienced. I learned that from time to time, we all experience failure or setback. It doesn't matter who you are; it doesn't matter what your economic status or whether you are black or white, male or female — you will experience setback at some point.

My mama used to say, "If you ain't failed yet, just keep living." I learned that with clarity, and a made up mind, no matter how far we fall, we can get back on track. Perhaps the greatest lesson of all I learned was that we are stronger than we think we are, and just when we think that we cannot go any further, a miracle will happen.

With every adversity, disappointment or failure comes an equal or greater opportunity to excel. In fact, as painful as my failure was, I eventually experienced joy and success that I never could have imagined. By accident I found a poem by Ralph Henry Thoreau in an old newsletter in a customer's trash basket. I stopped cleaning, read it and immediately decided to commit the words to memory and its principles to my heart. That poem marked a major turning point in my life. Here it is:

If one advances confidently
in the direction of his dreams,
and endeavors to live a life
which he has imagined,
he will meet with a success
that's unexplainable in common hours.
He will put some things behind,
pass an invisible boundary,
new, universal, more liberal laws
will establish themselves around and
within him — or the old laws will be expanded and interpreted
    in his favor
in a more liberal sense.
And . . . he will live with the license of a higher order of being.

To me, this poem says that if you only try, only start to live your life according to your highest dream, the universe will open up to you and everything that you attempt will work out in your favor.

I figured that I did not have anything to lose by putting this principle to test. Armed with the knowledge that I could confidently begin again, I developed a strategy to do just that. Get Good, Get Great, Get Going! is the result. It worked for me, and if you have suffered a major loss or setback — or simply need to change the way you are doing things, use this program as a source of inspiration to create success that is unexplainable in common hours!

Get Good

First, to get to unexplainable success, or success beyond your wildest dreams, you have got to get good — at getting good. Finding your purpose and making the quantum leap will help you to bridge the gap from failure to success.

Purpose

When we know our purpose, we will understand exactly who we are and why we were put on earth in the first place. In the '80s, we were goal-oriented. We wanted stuff . . . now! We had to have the big houses, the fancy cars, the right friends and the right places to see and be seen. Then came the constant turmoil and upheaval of the '90s and the dawn of the new millennium. Tired and stressed out, more and more people realized that enough was enough. No longer were we willing to work long, hard hours simply to buy more stuff. The quest to find purpose, to develop a stronger connection with out spiritual selves began to grow and reshape our lives. Many of us are now in transition, asking the question: What is purpose?

What is purpose? Purpose is your aim, your reason for being. In *Real Magic*, Dr. Wayne Dyer writes "When you are at purpose, you are truly flowing with life, experiencing a kind of harmony that comes from not having to strive for something else." Unfortunately, it usually takes a crisis, such as death, illness, divorce, job loss or some other kind of life-changing experience to force us to wake up and question life. Purpose helps us to discover who we are and where we are with our families, communities, our relationships, our work and our spiritual activities. Purpose shapes our legacy — that is, the imprint that we want to leave behind for all humanity. We cannot hope to find our purpose without first asking questions. The questions we ask or refuse to ask will determine the path that we take.

Life is a journey — a quest — so the question of purpose will not come up once, be answered and then last a lifetime. The question of purpose will come up about every ten years, during major life crises or transitions. In fact, if you look back and examine your life, you will see that for every transition in which you questioned your purpose, there was a period of upset, ambiguity and uncertainty. At each transition you asked the questions all over again: Who am I? What am I living for? Where am I going? How am I going to get there? What do I want to accomplish in life? What contributions or legacies do I want to leave behind?

Quantum Leap

To get good, we must first make a quantum leap! A quantum leap is an abrupt change in the way you do things. To make a quantum leap, we simply have to change the way we think about things. We must remove doubt and limitations. The quantum-leap theory allows us to multiply our level of effectiveness by cutting out all of the little things that slow us down. Typically, when we decide to try something different, we take baby steps, and little by little we reach our goals. I realized that in order to get "out of the toilets," I had to do something drastic. I could not just cut back on cleaning; I had to abandon it altogether in order to devote myself to a new career as a professional speaker. To do so, I had to see myself successful as a professional speaker. One day, I mentioned to one of my customers that I was a professional speaker. In a tongue-in-cheek manner she remarked, "So you're going to be known as 'the cleaning lady who speaks'?"

I said "No ma'm . . . but I will be 'the speaker who cleaned'!"

Off I went: I got business cards, developed a presentation and joined the Georgia Speakers Association long before I was ready to stand on a stage.

The quantum-leap theory, requires unconventional behavior. It requires taking uncommon action. Common sense focuses on obstacles. If you share an unconventional ideal with a limited-thinking friend, that friend's limited views will give you all the common-sense reasons you should not try to make the leap. Get rid of the "friend." That's what I did when I shared with a friend my belief that my destiny, my purpose in life was to become a speaker and help others with what I have learned, and she told me that I should stick to cleaning!

The quantum-leap theory forces you to think about what you want instead of what's reasonable. We must make quick, decisive moves when making a quantum leap. We can make up the difference when we have reached our goal. Making the quantum leap may not appear as neat and orderly as you would like; that's all right. The important thing is that you make the leap. Worry about perfection after you have made your point.

A good example is when I prepare my specialty, New Orleans'-style seafood gumbo. It is a long, drawn-out process that takes a long time and requires much attention. I use quite a few utensils, and when the gumbo is finally ready, the kitchen is a disaster, but my gumbo is always a hit. Afterwards . . . I clean up the kitchen.

Leap! What do you have to lose? In fact, when you leap, the movement will generate new ideas. Once you have figured out your purpose and made that quantum leap, you're good. Now, that you are good, s-t-r-e-t-c-h and Get Great.

GET GREAT!

Believe In You

The world discourages us when we want to try something new. There will always be people who will remind you of your shortcomings and past failures. Their warnings to play it safe or predictions that you can't do it are only their feelings of insecurities. Believe in you. See yourself where you want to be, and go for it. When you stretch and remove yourself from your normal place in the puzzle, it forces others to re-examine and question their own existence. That is not your problem. You cannot afford to stay back because others are not willing to do what it takes to move forward. The painful truth is as you progress and rebound, you will outgrow some of your old friends. Don't despair; they will be replaced by new friends with your same energy and vision.

I had a difficult time facing that reality. Unfortunately for me, some of my so-called friends did not only abandon me while I was trying to rebound, they also dropped me like a hot potato when I failed. As painful as it was, I am glad that it happened then. Now that I have come back, I put my love and energies into only those who loved and supported me unconditionally when they had nothing at all to gain.

To believe in yourself, you should also build your personal skills. Back up your belief in you with continuous learning. Make a commitment to yourself to become the best at what you want to be. Surround yourself with positive people; join organizations or groups that share your interest. Read everything you can about your area of interest.

Furthermore, observe the behavior of people who are successfully doing what you want to do. Study their behavior, and figure out what you are doing differently. Copy their behavior, and if you disagree, learn from their errors. I am a firm believer that the best way to learn is from other people's mistakes.

Also, create clarity for yourself by taking responsibility for figuring out your priorities and pointing yourself sharply in that direction. Your initiative will fuel the positive change you need. When I was struggling to survive by cleaning toilets, and trying to make the quantum leap to speaking, I could not keep up with many day-to-day chores. There were times when I had to make choices between spending money to attend a workshop or hiring a gardener to cut my grass. The workshops always won. I am sure that it did not make my neighbors too happy, but I figured if I became the speaker that I knew I could be, my yard would not be an issue.

Step out on faith! When you are in the middle of rapid change, your faith will help make the ambiguity and uncertainty manageable. Daily affirmations or bible readings can be just the balm you need to keep you grounded and rooted in the belief that you are on your divine path. In fact, a daily habit of spiritual renewal will work wonders on keeping on your path.

Stay focused. Don't let anything or anyone come between you and your dream. Focus is having the ability to apply all of your energies into your dream, without distraction. A good way to stay focused is to develop a visual picture of yourself successfully doing what you want to do. In my vision, I can see myself standing on stage in front of a large audience, and I am saying something that's so profound and touching that I have everyone's undivided attention. When I am finished, there is thunderous applause and a standing ovation. I can just see it! Now it's your turn: Get Going!

GET GOING!

Take Action

This is the hardest part of the process because this is where we are tested the most. Taking action means just that: Take action! Often people spend all of their time and energy getting ready to take action. They waste many hours or days preparing, getting organized and considering the options. You will never come up with a "perfect" solution. Just when you think that you have the perfect answer to a problem, like a moving target, the priorities have changed. My mama always says, "Study long, you study wrong." Nike's slogan says it best: "Just Do It!"

Some people are reluctant to take action for fear of failure. They mistakenly think that courage to take action is the absence of fear. Quite the contrary; courage is fear plus action. Failure is the greatest education of all. Failure is not a dead-end street, only a temporary detour.

Can you imagine taking a trip, only to get a few miles from your destination and running into a roadblock? What do you do? Do you turn around and go back home because of a roadblock? I doubt that. What you would probably do is ask for new directions or look at your map and try to figure out another way to reach your destination.

So it is with failure. When faced with an obstacle, don't give up; figure out another way to get there. A very dear friend of mine once said that he is afraid to fail, afraid to succeed and afraid to be mediocre. As a result, he does not do anything, thus ensuring that he will realize at least two of his fears. Having the courage to risk failure may not get you where you were initially headed, but it beats sitting at the starting line. One of my most popular presentations is one called "Cleaning Toilets and the Lessons Learned." In it I use humor while talking about bouncing back. I must admit that some of the things that were the most stressful to me when I was cleaning toilets now make very funny stories. I am so glad that I had the courage to keep going during my darkest times. I tell my audiences that I failed at making a living at cleaning, but now I get paid for speaking about it! Who would have thought that the most visible failure that I have ever suffered would be the catalyst for a whole new life of unexplainable success?

After struggling for five years to turn my life around, I found myself at my lowest point. I called my mama. My mama raised seven of us by herself in New Orleans, Louisiana, in one of the worst housing projects in the country. I knew that she had a lot of answers.

I said, "Mama, I'm so tired. Mama, I don't think that I can make it much longer. This is the worst that I have ever done."

Mama said "No baby . . . You done had worst times than these . . . Remember the shoes?"

I said "Shoes . . . Mama what do shoes have to do with anything????" Mama said, "Baby, you done forgot the shoes? Don't you remember the year that we had Hurricane Betsy, and we lost everything in the flood? And when it was time to go back to school you were afraid that you could not go because there was only one decent pair of shoes between you and your sister? But Thank God, the schools were on half day platoon schedule, so your sister wore the good shoes to school in the morning and you met her halfway at noon, and then you put the good shoes on and went on to school in the afternoon? Don't you remember that?"

I said "Oh, yeah Mama . . . that's right . . . I forgot about that! Oh, Mama, we were really poor, huh? Mama, how in the world did you do it? Did you ever get tired?"

Mama said "No baby, I just kept stepping."

"Mama, did you ever feel like giving up?"

"No baby, when God close a door, he open a window. I just kept stepping. . . ."

"Mama, does it ever get better?"

"Baby . . . it ALWAYS gets better . . . Just keep stepping!"

ABOUT
CONNIE PAYTON

*C*onnie Payton is The Cleaning Lady with a Message! From her expe-
*riences on the mean streets of New Orleans to the hallowed halls of
corporate America, from being labeled "not college material" in high
school to graduating with honors from Tulane University at 38, from a
career on the fast track with IBM to being downsized out after 15 years,
from being president of her own cleaning company to becoming the toilet
cleaner herself after her money ran out and she could not find quality staff,
Connie Payton can relate to people who want to break through. She is a
survivor who has been up and down and she says the view is much better
from the top!*

*A former award-winning marketing executive with IBM, Connie
combines her knowledge gained in corporate America with her experiences
in the toilets to deliver thought provoking presentations as a nationally recognized speaker and consultant. Connie's diverse background and vivid
storytelling help her paint pictures that everyone can relate to, while
encouraging her audiences to be resilient, resourceful and ready to bounce
back! Connie has been featured on radio and television interviews and was
a recent guest on "The Oprah Winfrey Show!"*

Contact information:
Connie Payton
5065 Rodrick Trail
Marietta, GA 30066
📞 (770) 516-9418

Back-yard Heroes: A Graduate-level Course on Leadership

By Gary Montgomery

Leaders know where they are going and how they are going to travel. They have defined their goals, but more importantly the emphasis is on the way they travel. Leaders model their beliefs by the way they live their lives. Their mission statement defines them.

My mission statement is very simple: to be the best husband and father I can be.

When I share this statement, I get that wrinkled-forehead look and comments like, "Is that all? Don't you want to accomplish more than that?"

I know others have guidelines for life that appear more noble and beneficial to humanity, such as to make the world a better place to live, or to lead the human race to greatness.

Well, I need a simpler statement — something a little more manageable.

I like my mission statement for three reasons: 1) It puts me in the statement; 2) it gives me a place to start, with instant results; and 3) it offers me additional benefits: If I become the best husband and father I can be, I'll also be the best person and leader I can be. That's what I'm shooting for: being the best I can be — the best person, the best manager, the best coach, the best leader, the best husband and the best dad.

It all started in my family, in my world, in my own back yard. My son Troy learned a simple message when he was thirteen, and fortunately I was there to watch, learn and grow with him.

Our back yard has always been a great place for our family. It's the place where we all play, learn and develop. There's a tree house in the old maple tree — not your run-of-the-mill tree house; this one is better classified as an upscale suspended condo. The enclosed area is eight by eight, with an additional eight-by-eight patio, and it's ten feet off the ground. My children hung a sign above the entrance: "Bad to the Bone." It's not what I had in mind, but it was their tree house.

Troy and I shared interesting and informative conversations building that tree house. We laughed and learned from each other, and I received more joy than a dad should be allowed to as I watched him and his friends share adventures, fun and overnights in that collection of wood and nails that sat in a place of honor in the back yard.

We also had a swimming pool in the back yard. My daughter, Tara, Troy and their friends did a lifetime of belly flops in that pool. It had a huge deck built around it, large enough to collect a crowd of neighbors. It was also just perfect for Mom and Dad to sunbathe and dream of what was to come for the youngsters in the water. And of course it was a perfect place for Tara and Troy to grow up, creating new dives and new strokes in the water as they yelled, "Mom! Dad! Watch this!"

And we did. We loved watching them.

The back yard also was a baseball field. Troy constructed it. He spent his own money to purchase a pitching machine that threw wiffle balls. He bought it to improve his hitting, but there's no reason you can't have fun while you learn.

Together we searched Louisville to find out where we could purchase plastic fencing used at construction sites. The bright yellow-and-orange fencing was stretched along the top of the deck railing to create the "orange monster," which was the left-field wall. A ball that cleared the wall had a good shot of landing dangerously close to anyone floating in the pool.

Right field was the side of the tree house, and our version of the "luxury box" was the deck, which extended from the tree house. We've seen a lot of fans watching from the right-field porch.

We named the field "Montgomery Field," after our family name. A friend of Troy's had the banner made at a sign company; it still hangs on the side of the tree house.

We also had a basketball court in the back yard for when the baseball field wasn't being used. That's where both Tara and Troy learned to shoot hoops. And that's where Bradley entered the back yard.

Bradley lived in the house behind us, just past the tree house. His back yard and ours connected, and he spent most of his time in our back yard because it was bigger — plus we had more toys!

Bradley's first venture into our back yard came just after his family moved in. Troy and I were shooting hoops and working on his game when we saw a little boy, four years old, sitting on his patio, watching us and wanting to be part of the fun. We invited him over.

From then on Bradley always seemed to show up anytime we were in the back yard, whether we were working or having fun.

When we threw a baseball, Bradley would come to the edge of his yard and sit down with his glove and baseball cap. He just watched . . . until Troy would invite him over.

We could tell Bradley loved to be part of our practice. He chased the ball when we missed it, but what he most looked forward to was when Troy showed him how to throw or catch. Bradley's mother, Tammy, said he would rather have Troy than anyone else teach him.

Bradley loved being part of our back-yard fun. He liked the entire Montgomery family: He liked my wife Judy because she gave him cookies; liked my daughter, Tara, because she baby-sat for him and his little sister; and he enjoyed being with me, calling me his first coach because I taught him the "give and go" on the basketball court. We called it Troy's favorite play. But Bradley's favorite person in the Montgomery family was Troy. Bradley idolized Troy.

One afternoon, as I pulled my car into the driveway, I could see Bradley in his back yard.

From the way he was looking at me, I could tell he wanted my attention. He didn't yell out, but he was swinging a baseball bat and then doing the play-by-play. "Crack. There it goes!"

Bradley obviously wanted me to notice him and the bat. As I walked across the yard I could see that the bat was brand-new — brand-new and just waiting to send a baseball deep, deep, deep to left field.

"Wow, is that a new bat?" I asked.

"Yes sir, Mr. Gary!" Bradley was beaming. "My Mom just bought it for me!"

Tammy, Bradley's mother, walked out her back door and onto the patio smiling. "He is so thrilled! He couldn't wait for you to see it."

I bent down on one knee, and together Bradley and I discussed the new bat. He showed me how to hold it and how to swing. We talked about how special it was and how many hits were on the way.

Bradley was clearly excited!

Later that afternoon Troy and I were in a hurry to get to baseball practice, and we were running behind time.

As we jumped in the car, ready to back out of the driveway, we saw Bradley again doing a play-by-play of his imaginary game.

"Crack! . . . Wow! Bradley hit that one a long way!"

"Troy," I said, "Bradley has a new bat."

"Dad, we don't have time," Troy said. "We have to get to practice."

"Just take a moment and check out his new bat."

Troy was reluctant, but he jumped out of the car. As Troy approached him, Bradley broke out a big smile. Troy bent down on one knee and shared Bradley's excitement.

Although I was still in the car, I was pretty sure I knew how the conversation was going. It was fun to watch Bradley when he was around Troy. He was animated and talkative, yet content to listen to every word Troy shared. Bradley obviously liked being the center of Troy's attention.

Tammy watched the two from behind her screen door, then stepped out onto the patio. She waved to me and spoke to both Troy and Bradley.

She later told me that she was so relieved that Troy thought the bat was a good bat because Bradley hadn't been sure — and that bat wasn't O.K. until Troy said it was O.K.!

After a few minutes Troy returned to the car, looking self-assured. I could tell he was pleased about what he had done.

"Bradley thinks a lot of you," I said to Troy as the car started down the driveway. I stopped before reaching the street and looked Troy in the eye. "Good job," I said to him. I thought Troy needed to hear that.

"Dad, you don't understand."

"I don't understand what?"

Troy was very serious now. "Dad . . . it's hard to be a hero."

I learned a lot that day. Yes, it's difficult to be a hero . . . especially in your own back yard, where people know you best. But if you can pull it off in the back yard, the qualities you acquire there will be with you when you travel the rest of the paths of life: in your social circles, in your family and in your career. Back-yard heroes make great leaders.

Heroes and leaders possess similar qualities, but foremost they attract individuals to be with them and follow them.

Troy displayed many of these leadership qualities with Bradley.

Leaders Step Up

Leaders aren't afraid to take a leadership role; in fact they welcome the opportunity.

I remember when my daughter finished her first season of softball. She was eight years old and had had a pretty good year of playing second base. As we drove home after the final tournament game, Tara was staring out the window, deep in thought.

"What's up, Beautiful?" I asked as we pulled out of the parking lot.

"Dad, I want to be the pitcher," Tara answered, still looking out the window.

"The pitcher?" It was the first time Tara had mentioned pitching.

"T-Bird, you're not a pitcher; it takes a lot of work to pitch."

"I want to pitch, Dad."

I explained that it took a lot of work to learn how to windmill pitch, more work than learning how to throw the ball over the plate for strikes. And being on the mound during a close game is pressure-packed: Some fans will be encouraging, but others might be jeering, hoping you fail.

I was hoping that she would decide it wasn't worth the effort. I didn't want her to come up short in her dreams. I was hoping she would set more attainable goals.

Yet, she persisted, still staring out the window, apparently thinking of what it would be like to be the pitcher.

Eventually I asked, "Why do you want to pitch?"

Tara turned, looked me in the eye and matter of factly explained, "Because everybody watches the pitcher."

Tara eventually became a pretty good pitcher during her career on the mound. She even tossed a no-hitter. But the main point is she welcomed a leadership role; in fact, she craved it.

Leaders step up. It's what they choose to do, even when those around them suggest they take a safer route.

Having the courage to step up to a challenge is a great quality. Leaders will do what has to be done: When it needs to be done, they step up. It's the first step to leadership.

Although leaders are sometimes anxious, sometimes uncertain, their nature is to confront situations and find solutions. They step up in the small issues so they are prepared for big issues. Others expect leaders to step up and make decisions. Sometimes leaders make incorrect decisions but apathy is not part of their resumé.

My father had a way of getting me to think about stepping up. He used to say, "Gary, do something, even if it's wrong." He wanted me to get started, to take the first step.

President Theodore Roosevelt's "Man in the Arena" is a great essay that illustrates the first step in leadership. He may have been thinking about back-yard heroes when he wrote it.

"It is not the critic who counts, not the one who points out how the strong man stumbled or how the doer of deeds might have done them better. The credit belongs to the man who is actually in the arena, whose face is marred with sweat and dust and blood . . . who, if he fails, at least fails while daring greatly, so that his place shall never be with those cold and timid souls who know neither victory nor defeat."[1]

Leaders always step up — on the softball diamond, in their careers and in the back yard.

Leaders Connect

Leaders connect with people: they build relationships.

I once coached a sixth-grader in football who was a coach's dream. He worked hard, did what was asked and was extremely positive.

But one day he changed. Bobby came to practice distracted. He wasn't trying, he wasn't listening and he didn't seem to care.

I was upset with Bobby and pulled him aside.

"What's wrong?"

He didn't answer. Instead he began to cry.

"Bobby, you have to tell me what's wrong. Let me help you."

Bobby continued to cry. I put my arm around him, and we sat down. Finally, he shared his problem.

"My dad left us." He said between tears. "He doesn't live with us anymore."

Bobby's world had been turned upside down. Football practice was no longer important.

We talked for a while, and I realized if I was going to help Bobby — to teach him, to lead him — I would have to get to know him — who he was and what he hoped to be. I had to ask questions and listen — listen to what he said and what he didn't say. To know Bobby I would have to explore with concern, and I would have to enter his world to relate to him. I wouldn't be able to coach Bobby, to lead him, to be his hero, until I had the desire to know his dreams and his fears — what made him happy and what turned that happiness to sadness.

It's necessary to know a person before you can build a relationship. That starts with communication on their terms. Leaders have to connect with individuals in a way which is important to them, in their world. Eventually leaders help individuals make the transition from their world to where they want to go — from where they are, to the goal.When we finished talking I turned toward the team and another realization struck me: No longer did I see a team of young men. I saw thirty individuals, all with stories to tell, just like Bobby. If I was still going to be their coach, their hero, their leader, I would have to get to know them as individuals.

Leaders are able to connect with their teams, or groups, one by one. They ask questions and then listen. They learn of individuals' dreams, joys and fears. Once they understand, really understand, they can take the next step.

Leaders Empower

Reggie Jackson, the Hall of Fame baseball player, offered a great recipe for a baseball manager. It's perfect for anyone interested in becoming a great leader.

"I'll tell you what makes a great manager: a great manager has the knack for making ballplayers think they are better than they think they are. He forces you to have a good opinion of yourself. He lets you know that he believes in you. He makes you get more out of yourself. And once you learn how good you really are, you never settle for playing anything less than your very best."[2]

Think about being forced to have a better opinion of yourself. That goes beyond empowerment.

Heroes and leaders help the people around them have better opinions of themselves. It works with spouses, children, coworkers, bosses, and friends. Once you help empower individuals to think better of themselves, to discover their talents, they will stick to you like Velcro. You will be their hero, and they will look to you for leadership.

In athletics, the great team leaders are the ones who make others better; consequently the entire team improves and prospers. That is real empowerment: trying to make others better.

It might be done purposely; in fact, you may not be aware of it for a while, but eventually it becomes second nature, as it did in the back yard with Troy and Bradley. Giving to people and knowing they are growing and developing will become second nature. It becomes part of you and actually becomes natural for you. Once individuals begin to grow when they are around you, they want to stay around you.

That's what back-yard heroes do. In a simple way they use great leadership techniques just by stepping up, building a relationship, and empowering others — making others feel good about themselves as they discover their talents.

It's a simple formula. Once you follow it and put it to use, it produces leaders. If you begin today to think of putting it to use with the people you connect with every day, it's like practice for athletes. By practicing, it becomes part of you. Great athletes don't have to think about diving for the ball; they do it, naturally. Leaders don't have to think about being heroes; they do it, naturally. It becomes part of you; it's the way you travel through life, it's living your mission statement.

When others prosper because they are around you, they'll call you a leader, but you'll understand you're just helping them reach the goals they have set for themselves. Leaders become heroes by helping others be the best they can be. Leaders step up, connect and empower. Leaders want to be heroes in all parts of their lives.

While watching Troy and Bradley bond, I realized I didn't have to sit in a classroom or in a seminar to learn how to apply leadership skills. Back yards are wonderful places to develop leaders. It's the best place I've found to practice being a hero and living out my mission.

(1) DiNunzio, Mario R. ed. Theodore Roosevelt. *An American Mind Selected Readings*. Penguin Books, 1995.

(2) Van Ekeren, Glenn. *Speakers' Sourcebook II Quotes, Stories, & Anecdotes for Every Occasion*. Prentice Hall: Englewood Cliffs, New Jersey, 1994.

ABOUT
GARY MONTGOMERY

Gary Montgomery is a television sportscaster, a coach and a professional speaker. He has been presenting to audiences and sharing his "I Can Play" attitude for over 20 years. Gary's stories and fun way of connecting to everyday life make it easy for companies and audiences to step up to leadership, enhance personal growth and improve their communication and presentation skills.

Contact information:
Prime Time Productions
Louisville, KY 40241
☎ (502) 339-0040
fax (502) 326-4942
e-mail: CoachGary@ICanPlay.com

LEADING FROM THE INSIDE OUT: NURTURE YOUR SELF-ESTEEM

By Curt Boudreaux, M.Ed.

Some perceive leaders as those who possess a position, title or wealth, and in some instances, this perception is absolutely true. However, leadership goes far beyond that. Leadership is not a place; it is a process. It is an action, not a position. Leadership is simply having an effect or influence on other people. In reality, a leader is anyone who impacts the lives of others by virtue of words and actions. Since we have the opportunity to do that on a daily basis, all are leaders in their own right, regardless of position or status in life.

Contrary to what many people believe, leaders are made, not born. Each of us has the inherent characteristics, the potential, to be an effective leader. It is our responsibility, however, to nurture and develop these characteristics in ourselves as well as in others.

One such characteristic is self-esteem. Oftentimes people use the terms self-concept and self-esteem interchangeably. Although closely related, the terms are different. Self-concept and self-image, though, are synonymous. That's the way we see ourselves based on information or feedback we get from others. Because of this information, we see ourselves a certain way and actually form a mental picture of who and what we are. Self-esteem, on the other hand, is the way we feel about that picture of ourselves that we see.

The word *esteem* means *value*. Literally, self-esteem is the degree to which we value ourselves and are able to recognize our worth as a person. A positive self-image translates into high self-esteem, and, conversely, a negative self-image produces low self-esteem.

The higher our self-esteem, the more positive influence we can have on others. There's an old saying that goes like this: "If you ain't got it, you can't give it." Once we are able to see the goodness and worth in ourselves, we are able to see it in others, too. As our self-esteem grows, we are able to support and encourage the development of talent and abilities in others. At this point we have truly put on the mantle of leadership.

A healthy self-esteem increases our effectiveness and allows us to be more productive and, ultimately, more successful in our personal and professional lives. Yet, this is not a short-term project; it is a life-long process. We must work constantly to build and enhance our self-esteem. Some basic esteem builders which we should be aware of are attitude, belief in self and confidence. Let's examine each of these more closely since they provide a solid foundation on which to build our self-esteem.

ATTITUDE

Attitude is the way we view life and everything in it and how we respond to that view. It's a feeling or an emotion that we have toward something or someone. Attitude is crucial for success since it determines our altitude — how high and how far we will go in life. Studies reveal that eighty-five percent of the people who get good jobs, keep them and receive promotions do so because of a positive attitude.

Our beliefs and thoughts determine our attitudes — thoughts for the short term, beliefs for the long haul. They dictate how we feel about ourselves, about others or about a situation. These feelings, in turn, prompt an action or behavior, which always produces a consequence or result. The result then reinforces the original belief, thus making it stronger and more deeply rooted. This process is rewarding if the belief is positive — but devastating if negative. How it works is illustrated in the "Behavior Cycle" at right.

The Behavior Cycle

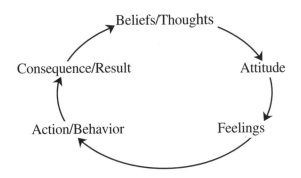

Positive (+) or Negative (-)

Note that the cycle can be positive or negative depending upon our belief or prevailing thought. If our belief system, what we truly believe about ourselves, is positive, then our overall attitude will be positive over a long period of time. Yet what determines our attitudes at any given moment is our thoughts. The mind is capable of holding hundreds, perhaps even thousands, of thoughts during the course of a day but only one at a time. That one thought per moment determines our attitude at the moment. If that thought is positive, then our attitude is positive. Similarly, a negative thought produces a negative attitude.

What is crucial to remember is that since we can choose our thoughts, we can choose our attitudes. Vicktor Frankl, in his book *Man's Search For Meaning*, says that "Man's greatest freedom is to be able to choose his attitude in any given set of circumstances." We can't control what happens to us, but we can control our response to it. That's attitude.

Psychologists tell us that ninety-eight percent of the way we feel each day is determined by the decision we make relative to how we're going to feel. It's our choice. What did you say when you woke up this morning: "Good morning, Lord!" or "Good Lord, it's morning!"? Same basic words, but each phrase reveals a totally different attitude.

Our attitude stands out every day. People can easily determine whether our attitudes are positive or negative after just a few minutes of conversation. Attitude even comes through over the telephone. Our words, and perhaps more importantly, our tone of voice speak volumes to others about our attitude.

As a motivational speaker, I use the telephone as a means of conveying attitude and enthusiasm. I have fun with it. It began several years ago with the message on my answering machine. I recorded the usual message but ended with a positive one, such as, "Whether you think you can or think you can't, you're right."

Several months later I changed the ending to "Make yourself a great day!" My wife, Sue, commented, "Curt, that doesn't make sense."

"Of course it does," I replied. "The subtle message is that your day will be exactly what you choose to make it to be. You're the architect of your day and can design it according to your own specifications."

Then I became even more creative. I decided to take my usual message and create a rap song. Now, if someone calls my home, this is what he or she will hear on the answering machine:

Yo! You've reached the Motivation Man, and my name is Curt
You know I'll call you back soon 'cause I'm always alert.
Leave your name and your number when you hear the beep
and stay close to your phone 'cause I never really sleep!

I believe in commitment, so I'll call back in a hurry
Let the Motivation Man take away all your worry.
So relax and be cool and leave your message in a plan
'Cause you're in good hands with the Motivation Man!

Sue's reaction to my rap song was, "My God! Who in the world is going to hire you after listening to that?"

I responded, "I don't know, but at least they'll know that I have a positive attitude and a sense of humor — and that I am enthusiastic about what I do." This unique message has created memorability for me and some people call specifically to listen to it.

One of the leading psychologists of the twentieth century, William James, said "The greatest discovery of my generation is that human beings can alter their lives by altering their attitude of mind." Not only can we change our lives, but we can also change the lives of others. People enjoy working and associating with those who have a great attitude. Begin choosing positive thoughts and building a solid belief system today. If you do, you will develop a great attitude, enhance your self-esteem and exert a positive influence on others.

Attitude Boosters

1. Choose positive thoughts.

2. Monitor your talk. Identify the positive and negative words you use. Make a focused effort to eliminate the negative words from your vocabulary.

3. Verbalize only the positive. Try it for one day — not a single negative remark. See what a difference it makes.

4. Choose a positive perspective. See the "bright side" of things by turning unpleasant events into opportunities.

5. Accept each day as a fresh start, either to continue yesterday's successes or to begin again with a new resolve in making changes.

BELIEF IN SELF

Another means of building self-esteem is to believe in yourself. Belief in self means having faith in yourself and your abilities. Being "sold" on yourself is the cornerstone of success because you actually become what you believe about yourself. As one aphorism affirms, "The me I see is the me I'll be."

If you see yourself as a winner, you will think, talk, walk and act like a winner. In essence, you become a winner. Conversely, the opposite is true if you see yourself as a loser. Incidentally, being a winner doesn't mean being better than or doing more than someone else; it simply means being the best that you can be. You compare what you are doing in life to what you are capable of doing, or your potential. You are in competition with only yourself, no one else.

Mahatma Ghandi said, "If I believe I cannot do something, it makes me incapable of doing it. But when I believe I can, then I acquire the ability to do it, even if I did not have the ability in the beginning." These are powerful words that clearly express the importance of believing in yourself.

Each of us possesses certain beliefs about self which are the result of information accumulated from others since birth. We have been told certain things about ourselves often enough that we have come to accept them as true, whether they are or not. It is important to understand that some of these beliefs may be not only inaccurate, but totally false. It is crucial that we rid ourselves of faulty, negative beliefs because they become our reality. The body manifests what the mind harbors.

All information received through the five senses is stored in our subconscious mind. Like a sponge, our minds soak in everything. The mind, however, does not make value judgments. To the subconscious mind, the information is neither right nor wrong, simply information which it processes. An abundance of tainted information creates a negative belief system, which invariably produces undesirable results.

Exposure to negativism on a regular basis has a detrimental effect on our belief system by virtue of its entrance into our subconscious mind. Complaining, gossiping, vulgarizing and repeating negative thoughts are damaging and should be avoided at all costs. According to Earl Nightingale, "You must be careful what you allow to enter your mind because your mind is like a garden. It will grow whatever is planted." There can and will be no variance from this. Know that you will reap exactly what you sow.

Fortunately, we need not remain the way we are now. We can change our beliefs or "reprogram" ourselves with the tools of positive self-talk, visualization and affirmation.

Self-talk is the words we say to ourselves, about ourselves — both silently and aloud. As such, they permeate our subconscious mind. When we use positive self-talk — that is, saying and thinking good things about ourselves — we nurture ourselves. At this point we become our best friends instead of our worst enemies.

Visualization or imaging is creating a mental picture of something or someone. You actually "see" it in your mind. Napoleon Hill said, "Whatever the mind can conceive and believe it can achieve." See yourself the way you want to be, and your subconscious mind will receive this powerful visualization. Since the mind cannot tell the difference between a real experience and a vividly imagined one, it will work fervently to bring it to reality. See yourself as a good, kind, capable, loving and successful person who impacts others in a powerful, positive way.

An affirmation is a positive thought consciously placed in the subconscious mind, through repetition, to produce a desired result. It has three components: first person, present tense and positive language. Always use "I" and the present tense when constructing an affirmation. For the subconscious mind, the past and future are nonexistent. All it knows is now. Always use positive terms, too. Using positive language conditions the mind and builds a strong belief system.

Using affirmations ensures that you are filling your mind with positive messages. You can also record them on audio tape and listen at your leisure. You need not consciously listen to them. As long as you can hear them, they are reaching the subconscious mind for storage and use. When recording affirmations, use much feeling and emotion.

Several years ago, after reading some books on the subconscious mind, I decided to test this intriguing theory by conducting my own experiment. I enlisted the help of my wife for this project. Sue is a skilled bowler who has been bowling in a league for 25 years, since the age of twelve. I asked her to tell me some things she would like to achieve in bowling but, as of yet, had not. She replied that she would like to maintain an average of 165 (her average at the time was 156), to consistently bowl games in excess of 200 and to bowl a 600 scratch series in league play.

I developed several scripts on self-esteem and believing in oneself, using very positive language. Then I developed some affirmations, using information from these scripts as well as from Sue's "wish list." Here are some of the affirmations exactly as they were used: "I like who I am, and I feel good about myself." "I am successful, and I am a winner in all aspects of my life." "I am an excellent bowler, and I am maintaining an average of 165." "I am an excellent bowler, and I am consistently bowling 200+ games." "I am an excellent bowler, and I am bowling a 600 scratch series." These were followed by more general, positive affirmations, both in number and in content.

The next step was for me to record the information on audio tape. The scripts were recorded first, followed by the affirmations. When recording affirmations, each one was to be repeated three times. After all were recorded, each one was to be repeated an additional time, substituting "you" for "I." For example: "You like who you are and you feel good about yourself." This has the effect of someone else affirming what you are saying about yourself.

Sue began listening to this tape two or three times a day. When she was bowling, I encouraged her to repeat an affirmation as she stepped up to the line and asked her to visualize the ball going down the alley and knocking down all of the pins. Six days later she called from the bowling alley to inform me that she had just bowled a 603 scratch series — her first ever!

For some reason, several days later she stopped listening to the tape, so I played it every morning while she was sleeping in order for the information to enter her subconscious mind. Three weeks later she bowled a 608 and a 630 scratch series on consecutive Tuesday nights. Sue consistently bowled 200+ games during league play and ended the season with a 164 average, just one pin below her target score. At one point her average reached 170.

Now for the obvious question: Did the tape improve Sue's bowling skills? Absolutely not. What it did do, however, was remove the psychological limitations she had placed on herself relative to what she could accomplish. Ordinarily, she would position herself to bowl well, and when the time came to roll the strikes or spares needed to produce the desired score, her negative self-talk and beliefs would kick in — phrases like: I'm not good enough, I don't deserve it, I don't have the ability, I can't, and so forth. Her self-sabotage was destructive and defeating. However, by reversing that negative thinking, her true ability was able to surface, creating the desired results.

This experiment illustrates how we can reverse our thinking and beliefs to get what we want. Believe in yourself, and you will become the winner you were meant to be. You will accomplish and achieve much more than you ever imagined possible and will truly begin to tap into your potential. People will turn to you for guidance and direction, and, when they do, you will be able to share with them the simple tools you used to make a difference in your life. By so doing, you will make an appreciable difference in their lives, too.

Belief Builders

1. See yourself as you can be, not as you are.

2. Make a list of what you believe about yourself. Concentrate on the ones that build your esteem and promote success.

3. Use the tools of self-talk, visualization and affirmation to reverse negative beliefs about yourself.

4. Encourage, support and nurture positive beliefs in others.

5. See the best in others, and focus on their innate goodness.

CONFIDENCE

A third method for building self-esteem is self-confidence. This is the assurance of one's ability or feeling sure of oneself. Confidence is developed by taking positive risks, attempting a task with no guarantee of success and actually having the distinct possibility of failing. Start with small tasks in order to experience success, and use them as stepping-stones and building blocks to larger and more challenging ones. Success breeds success. There is nothing like it to build confidence.

You must learn to take risk. In baseball, it's impossible to steal second base with one foot clinging to first. One of three things can happen in an attempted steal: You might get picked off at first; you may get thrown out at second; or you might be successful in your effort to steal second base. However, you will never know unless you step off the bag and take the risk. The same is true in life. Playing it safe leaves you "holding" the bag.

Understand that it takes courage to take a risk. Also, contrary to what many people believe, courage is not the absence of fear. No! Courage is being afraid to do something but doing it in spite of your fear. Cus D'Amato, a famous boxing trainer, said, "Heroes and cowards are acted upon by the same fear. They just respond differently." The hero advances while the coward retreats.

We are born with only two fears: the fear of falling and the fear of loud noises. All the rest of our fears are learned and, through repetition, are driven deep into our subconscious minds where they begin to dictate, dominate and control our beliefs and, ultimately, our actions. Our fears assume control and prevent us from taking risks. What are some of these fears? There is the fear of failure, of success, of ridicule and of criticism from the "horn honkers." Who are the horn honkers? The following illustrates:

A lady was driving down Canal Street in New Orleans. She stopped for a red traffic light, and as she did, her car engine died. She tried in vain to start it. Her second attempt failed as well. By this time the traffic light turned green. The man in the car behind her honked his horn. Another effort on her part proved just as futile as before. Honk, honk, honk came the sound from the car behind her. By now she had flooded the engine and would be going nowhere. The impatient man behind her just sat on his horn — hoooooooooonnnnk! The lady very calmly stepped out of her car, walked to the rear and said to the driver, "Excuse me, sir. If you would be so kind as to try to start my car for me,

I'd be more than happy to sit here and honk your horn for you!"

The world is full of horn honkers. They are the spectators of life who sit in the bleachers and complain, criticize and condemn but never, ever get into the game themselves — because they lack courage. So why worry about them? Go ahead and take a risk. As Ann-Margaret's character, Ariel, says in the movie *Grumpy Old Men*, "The thing you'll regret most about life is the risks you weren't willing to take." Don't have any regrets: take the risk.

Fear causes us to want to stay in our comfort zone. That's the place in our mind where we feel safe, secure, unthreatened and prepared. Our comfort zone becomes larger or smaller, depending upon our willingness to risk. It can be as small as a postage stamp or as large as the world, relative to our level of confidence. However, staying in our comfort zone causes us to become stagnant. On the other hand, stepping out creates growth and increases our self-esteem and ability to influence others.

I have learned that the best way to overcome fear is to face it. As a young boy in elementary school, I was deathly afraid to speak in front of a group. I was so shy I couldn't lead a group in silent prayer. Yet, I was elected 4-H club president in both fifth and sixth grades. I dreaded the meetings. With my heart racing, hands clammy and voice quivering, I reluctantly stood before the club members and conducted the meetings. I hated every minute and was relieved when it was over. That experience caused me to dodge those kinds of situations for years.

I successfully avoided speaking in front of groups until my senior year in college. I intentionally postponed the dreaded speech class as long as I could, but it was inevitable. I struggled through it and managed to survive, yet I still didn't like it. Not only did I feel the trauma as I was giving the speech, but also for many hours prior to it. I was miserable.

Ironically, as I began my teaching career, I was never nervous in front of the students. Yet, with the faculty, fear took charge. Knowing I wanted to make a point or comment at a faculty meeting, the same physical maladies from the 4-H experience would haunt me. Speaking in public was still difficult for me as an adult, but I knew at some point I must face it.

I began to volunteer for tasks that required me to address groups of people. These included leadership positions in civic and professional organizations, making presentations to other school faculties and serving as a lector in my church. The more I did it, the less nervous I became. One day I noticed I was not only not nervous; I was actually enjoying it! Only because I faced my fear and would not allow it to defeat me was I able to overcome that fear.

The irony is that today I am a professional speaker. Do I still have "butterflies" before a speaking engagement? Occasionally. As a speaker, though, the key is not to be rid of the butterflies but to have them fly in formation.

A ship is safe in a harbor, but that is not the purpose for which it was built. We, like the ship, must leave port and travel unknown waters. We must take the risk. That is how we grow and develop our self-confidence, and at the same time, build our self-esteem. Doing so, in turn, empowers us to be leaders and positively affect others.

Confidence Creators

1. Make a list of the risks you took this past year and how they turned out.

2. Determine what you learned and how you grew from each one, regardless of the outcome.

3. Recall the opportunities you had to take a risk in the last year and did not take. Next to each one, write the reason you failed to try.

4. Resolve to take all reasonable risks from this point on if they are in your best interest.

5. Encourage and support others to follow your example and become risk-takers.

Your self-esteem will soar as you improve your attitude, believe in yourself and develop confidence. You will become a role model for those around you and exercise the kind of influence that makes a difference in your life. This happens when you take the initiative to improve yourself. When you do, you will become the kind of person others will want to emulate and follow. At this point, you are truly leading from the inside out.

ABOUT
CURT BOUDREAUX, M.ED.

---

*C*urt Boudreaux, M.Ed., known as the Motivation Man, is a motivational speaker, author, and Cajun humorist. He works with individuals who want to improve the quality of their lives and with companies and organizations who want their people to realize their potential. His keynotes and seminars explore the topics of high-level self-esteem, positive and profitable attitudes, and irresistible leadership.

Curt is the author of The ABC's of Self-Esteem *and* Never Kiss An Alligator on the Lips! *Additionally, he is a contributing writer for* Personal Excellence *magazine and has recorded the two audio tape series, "The Keys to Unlocking Your Potential" and "Never Kiss An Alligator on the Lips!" He is a member of the National Speakers Association and a past president of the New Orleans Speakers Association.*

Contact information:
The Motivation Man
P.O. Box 422
Golden Meadow, LA 70357
(📞) (504) 632-6177
fax (504) 632-4898
e-mail: CurtBoudreaux@cajunnet.com
web: www.nolaspeaks.com/cb

GROWING WITHIN TO WIN

By Gayle Lantz

My three-year-old daughter dashed in front of the other children on a preschool field trip, and as she made her way to the front of the line, she proudly exclaimed, "I'm the weeder!" Obviously she'd meant "leader." At such a young age she was already exhibiting traits that many in the corporate world believe it takes to become a leader.

There's an interesting coincidence in calling herself a "weeder." What my daughter will eventually learn is that leaders are weeders. They are accomplished at removing those things in their lives that prevent them from growing, and are also adept at finding rich soil and healthy climates that foster their lifelong learning and development. Ultimately, successful leaders are growers.

In this chapter we will explore ways to foster your own personal and professional growth to become the leader you want to be. It is a process with several steps. Like good gardeners, let's start with weeding.

W-E-E-D ing

Work on who you are, not what you do. Leaders know themselves well.

We've all been through training or classes that help us to do things better — manage our time more efficiently, learn new technology, develop new skills. However, if we perfect our skills without having a clear sense of who we are, we may become highly skilled, unfulfilled workers. And that does not translate into good leadership. Simply put, to lead others, it is important to first have a strong sense of who you are.

When we consider the notion of who we are, we must remain aware that our experiences have a profound effect on our perception of ourselves. For example, if we've had a long career in the corporate world, it's easy to forget who we were before we began that career. We may base our self-worth on the feedback we get in an annual review, on sales results, on the number of hours we work in a day, or on how much money we make. With that kind of thinking, we're being unfair to ourselves.

To gain better perspective, you may want to consider using some assessment tools. There are many different kinds on the market that measure everything from psychological types and career interests to innate abilities and managerial styles. Take advantage of any testing instruments offered through your company or local college or university. Part of confirming who we are is admitting what we're not. Testing can be a helpful and revealing tool in the process.

To discover yourself, peel back layers that have been accumulating over the years. Forget your company's mission statement for the time being and reflect on your own mission statement. Do you have one? And if you do, are you being true to it?

Eliminate your title. Leaders are not concerned with their status.

Although society has conditioned us to think in these terms, you should stop thinking of yourself as your position or title. It's easy and comfortable to refer to yourself as "an account executive," "a manager," or "a vice president." However, these titles don't really mean anything. It is more difficult to explain what we do, what it means to us, or more importantly, what our goals are than to simply offer a title.

Another pitfall is the fact that we usually share what we've already done, as opposed to what we want to do. For example, individuals who seek new job or career opportunities often focus too much on where they've been instead of where they would like to go. Consider a typical resume: It has one summary statement or objective statement and one or two pages devoted to past experience.

Students also tend to define themselves based on the past instead of the future, possibly because they are frequently asked, "What was your major?" or "Where did you go to school?" Hear the difference between "I am a business major" versus "I would like to explore marketing and influence how people buy products."

Leaders talk about the difference they would like to make, not the position they would like to have or the things they have already done. Give it a try by completing this sentence:

I am now no longer a _____. You are just you. Do you recognize yourself?

Empty your trash. Leaders don't dwell on negatives.

Get rid of the negative relationships, commitments or influences in your life. Pluck the dead leaves. Stay clear of critics, whiners and doubters.

Critics find fault with everything.

Whiners complain about everything.

Doubters don't believe in anything.

Most people don't mean to be negative. In fact, many think they are being helpful to you. They believe they are doing you a favor by helping you see all sides of a situation — the reality. But often they're simply reflecting their own fears and insecurities about change. In turn, they unintentionally keep you from growing.

Are you engaged in work that helps you grow — or work that burns you out? Stop doing those things that drain you, and seek opportunities that offer new growth. Commit to focusing on the positive. For example, if you've had a tough day, don't come home and relive all the things that went wrong. My husband and I used to have daily competitions over dinner to see who had the most miserable day. Each topped the other's story with a description of a situation that was even more infuriating or stressful than the last. By the time we'd finished dinner, we felt exhausted, frustrated and defeated. We both lost.

Toss those nagging negative thoughts into your mental disposal. Instead of regurgitating all the problems and stress of the day, ask yourself what you are learning from the experiences and how they can move you forward. Eventually you'll find yourself developing habits that create more positive results.

Dig deeper. Leaders lead themselves.

Make an effort to think differently about what you want and why you want it. What really motivates you? What makes you tick? What are your values? How will you take charge of your own life? This is called self-leadership. You must master it before you can lead others effectively. However, be aware that self-leadership involves challenge and risk.

Some individuals purposely choose to challenge themselves by experiencing something unique and different. They intentionally lead themselves out of their comfort zones to experience things that are new, creative, thought-provoking or unusual. They may experience another culture or another way of life. Doing something "out of the norm" stimulates their growth and deepens their sense of purpose in the world. It also helps them better understand others. With this new perspective and understanding, they become even better leaders.

Sometimes stepping out of your comfort zone requires taking a break from what you are currently doing. Take Mel, for example. She decided to take some time off from her high-pressure, lucrative position in the pharmaceutical industry. After leaving her position for a few months, she realized how much more rewarding it was to work in a different environment and do something she believed in. Before she landed a permanent position, Mel got a taste of work in a variety of fields by taking on temporary positions. Although overqualified for these positions, she gained valuable experience, ruled out some possibilities and became more focused. This insight will allow Mel to make better decisions for the rest of her professional life.

Work can be a fulfilling expression of your true self and what matters most to you. During your career, you will likely hold as many as eight different positions in at least five different organizations. You are also likely to change fields altogether at least twice. Leaders view such change as an opportunity rather than as an endurance test. They navigate the twists and turns while keeping focus on their goal — which is to do something they find genuinely rewarding. Goals may shift over time, but change is accepted as part of the growth process. In essence, successful leaders manage their own careers wisely.

Finding Good S-O-I-L

Now that we have weeded out what often holds us back, it is time to grow. However, we all know that nothing grows in a vacuum. In order to grow, we need the right environment and nutrients. Whether you seek out new soil or you want to cultivate your own where you are, you have a choice. Think of it as good S-O-I-L in which you can grow personally and professionally.

Seek out positive people. Leaders enlist the help of others in their journey toward their goal.

You can gain a tremendous amount of energy from other people. Work hard to find mentors, advocates and cheerleaders:

Mentors offer guidance and coaching.

Advocates can actually take action on your behalf, such as picking up the phone and making a connection for you.

Cheerleaders believe in you just because you're you; it doesn't matter if you win or lose.

All of these three types of people are critical to your own growth and success as a leader. Stay in touch with them as much as possible.

Open your mind. Leaders believe in possibilities.

Do you ever hear that voice in your head saying, "I can't do that because . . ."

"If only I had an advanced degree . . ."

"If only I were younger or older or had more time or more money, then I could do it."

"If only . . . (you fill in the blank)"?

What's holding you back? These types of thoughts kill your potential before it can even develop.

Practice listening to yourself, and be aware when these thoughts creep up. Consciously replace them with thoughts of "I can because . . ." and "I will because . . ." It's not easy at first, but if you believe enough in what you want to do, be or accomplish, you can conquer those voices with a mind that's open to possibilities.

Imagine what you want to be. Leaders see the goal before they attain it.

Your imagination can be a powerful tool in self-leadership. If you can picture yourself in a place, doing what you want to do in the way you want to do it, you're on your way to getting yourself there.

Some may interpret this visualization as "leaders always know where they are going." However, the truth is that even if they don't know where they are going, they're trying to figure it out. Remember that leadership is not inborn, and these individuals are clarifying their vision as they go along. Leadership is a developmental process. It is acquired through experience. What separates leaders from the rest is their willingness to take risks, learn from them and continue to shape the future as they see it.

You see, leaders become irresistible when they are not trying to attract followers, but when they seek to be their personal best and follow their own vision. This freedom and commitment allow them to grow in ways that naturally attract others as they are moving toward their own goals. The clearer the vision, the more likely the leader will achieve his or her goals and capture the imaginations of others who want to grow as well.

Learn as you go. Leaders don't have to have all the answers.

Learning is an active process. If you master the art of learning from both positive and negative experiences, you will accomplish more than most. Leaders reflect on their experiences and take from them knowledge that can propel them toward their goal. Sometimes it takes repeating the same mistakes, but if you eventually identify something about yourself that is contributing to the misstep, you will grow.

Here's an example: Jack was an excellent salesperson, one of the friendliest team members, full of energy and highly motivated.

However, under certain circumstances, he could not handle pressure, which in turn resulted in explosive situations in the office. Time after time he lashed out at others in highly stressful situations. After getting feedback from others, he became more aware of his actions. Over time, he was able to change his behavior by learning to laugh at himself. By not taking himself so seriously, Jack learned to manage potentially difficult situations more gracefully. His actions naturally reflected the lighter side of himself he had discovered.

One of the most important keys to recognizing flaws and learning to change them is to stop blaming others. Instead, take a hard look at what you might be doing — or not doing — that is contributing to the problem. Strive to address it. Leaders are learners who take responsibility for what their experiences teach them.

So now we know ideal soil is a place filled with positive influences — a place that allows you to explore possibilities and follow your vision. It's also a place that fosters your learning.

Does your current employer offer the environment you need?

Now that you have an idea of what you need to grow and succeed, ask yourself if you can grow in your current position or with your current employer. The truth is, leaders don't plant themselves where they cannot grow. How do you decide where you need to be?

Take risks. Test the waters to see how receptive your company is to your ideas about professional growth and increasing your contribution to the company (regardless of your level or status with the company). More progressive companies understand the value of finding creative ways to develop their leaders. They realize that if the climate or circumstances are not right for top talent, that talent leaves, especially in a strong economy. Organizations want to know how to retain high achievers. Don't search for new soil until you've tried to cultivate your own where you are.

Companies are now being encouraged to initiate discussions with key employees to understand their personal and professional goals. They engage in a collaborative process where communication is clear and open. The employer then becomes an integral part of the process in that leader's growth. In turn, they both reap the benefits. However, as mentioned before, if companies do not demonstrate this type of commitment, they run the risk of losing excellent leaders. Because leaders do not stay in a job without growth opportunity, they move toward their own goals and attract new followers.

Kate is a perfect example. She had an unfulfilling job in a brokerage company. However, she was very good at her work and extremely loyal to her manager. The thought of a change made her feel guilty because she knew that her manager and others in the office relied heavily upon her. Although her work was outstanding, she had become overqualified and wanted to grow professionally. By honestly assessing who she was, what she liked and didn't like about her work and what skills, personality and interests she possessed, she eventually made the decision to leave.

Kate remained with the same employer but took a new position in a different city. She was surprised to discover the strong leadership skills she possessed but was unable to employ in her previous position. Now that she perceives herself as a leader, she will continue to grow as a leader. She will not only be more fulfilled herself, but will also have a greater capacity to help others grow.

You've done your weeding and found your soil. Now you can grow. Here are a few truths that should help you along the way:

Passion ignites the growth process. Having spent many years in the retirement planning industry, I was accustomed to asking people, "What do you want to do when you retire?" Now as a career coach, I ask, "What do you want to have accomplished when you retire?" Leaders can answer this question with conviction. They understand the difference between living for a pension and living for a passion. Their passion is the key to making a difference and determines the direction of their own personal and professional growth.

Growth is a challenging and complex process. I once gave a speech comparing the growth process to the experience of pregnancy.

You know something is developing inside you and you're going through different stages that at times are weighty, awkward and strange. It may be uncomfortable and exciting at the same time. You may not know what to expect, but you accept the challenge of extending yourself beyond what you thought was originally possible. Leaders have expanded visions of themselves that enable them to achieve more based on their own goals, values and understanding of themselves.

Growth is essential to making a difference. By knowing clearly who you are, what you believe in and what you can contribute, you prepare yourself for whatever life has to offer and, more importantly, for what you can bring to life. It's a process that takes time, patience and conviction. Deciding to grow takes a commitment to yourself and to others. As you commit yourself to becoming the best person you can be, you are also committing yourself to offering more to others.

So often we see would-be leaders simply trying to win the race, climbing the corporate ladder or vying for that next promotion. They are aggressive, but without purpose, solid values or real personal insight. Then there are others, who like children playing tag, wait for someone to tag them and say, "You're it!" They hope or believe the company or someone will recognize their talent and leadership potential.

The mature leader understands that leadership requires insight and growth that goes beyond trying to get ahead of others or waiting to be recognized. Good leadership is not about getting ahead but growing within — developing who you are, confirming what's most important to you, then acting in ways that are consistent with your own goals.

Keep weeding through those things in your life that prevent you from being your best self. Keep digging until you find the best soil. Once you do, you will find yourself in a garden of possibilities. And you will see how positively you can influence those around you. Plant yourself firmly in a place that gives you the greatest opportunity for personal and professional growth. There you will find the leader within yourself ready to make a difference.

ABOUT
GAYLE LANTZ

Gayle Lantz is President of WorkMatters, a career coaching company that works with individuals who want to take charge of their careers and organizations that want to develop leaders. Gayle's professional background includes extensive experience in the mental health field. This unique combination of experiences gives her the precise tools necessary to work with those in search of personal and career direction. And many have relied on Gayle's expertise and guidance in the areas of career focus, transition and advancement strategies.

Gayle is a member of the International Association of Career Management Professionals, the International Coach Federation and the National Speakers Association. In addition to career coaching, Gayle speaks to groups of all sizes about career enhancement, professional growth and related issues.

Contact information:
WorkMatters
104 Peachtree Road
Birmingham, AL 35213
𝒞 (205) 879-8494
fax (205) 879-9818
e-mail: Lantz@mindspring.com

BEE a Leader

By Kathy B. Dempsey

Nope and Hope Bee were both sitting around watching TV one night when a news flash interrupted their favorite program, Wheel of Honey. "We interrupt this broadcast to bring you a special news report. In a conclusive study just out today, scientists have proven without a doubt that bees cannot fly," the announcer proclaimed. "Flying for a bee is aerodynamically impossible!" In shock, the Bees gazed at each other and said, "Now what do we do?"

Nope and Hope both heard the same message. Now they were faced with the age-old question, "To BEE, or not to BEE?" Dejectedly, Nope said, "I can't fly like a bird or soar like an eagle. I can't do it like they can. They say we can't fly. I guess they are right."

Undaunted, Hope responded, " I do not care what anyone else says, even those expert scientists. I don't care if they say my body is too large for my wings. I know my mission in life is to fly. And I will fly anyway!"

Nope, unfortunately, listened to the scientists and all the negative "you can't fly" talk. And he didn't fly, instead wasting his life away, not living up to his full potential and spending many years stumbling about. Many of Nope's friends also stopped flying. On the other hand, Hope defied all physical laws and began to fly, reaching places she never thought she could reach and taking many of her friends with her.

Now, Nope and Hope were both bees who affected other bees' lives in many ways. And so it is with people. We are all leaders. Leaders are not just managers and executives. All of us, every day, affect other people's lives in many ways. The question is not if we are leaders, but how, and in what direction we choose to lead.

My greatest lesson in leadership came not from a textbook but from personal adversity.

The year was 1987. They told me I was going to die. I was 26 years old. At the time, I was working as a nurse at a psychiatric hospital in Chattanooga, Tennessee. While sitting in the office one bright sunny afternoon, the phone rang. "Hello, Kathy, this is Dr. Gazaleh." Hesitantly, he said, "I . . . I am sorry to tell you this over the phone but . . . your HIV test . . . it's come back positive. We need you to come to my office at the hospital right away."

As I hung up the phone, my heart sank. I was in shock. My worst nightmare had come true: I had been exposed to an AIDS patient while working in the emergency room at the county hospital twelve months prior. Because of the exposure, the doctors had decided to test me every three months for a year. After three negative tests, I thought I had nothing to worry about, but I couldn't have been more wrong.

Immediately, I rushed to the hospital. My head was spinning. I couldn't think. My hands were shaking visibly; I could barely grip the steering wheel. This just couldn't be true. Why me? I was a nurse — trying to help a patient. I was not ready to die! I was in the prime of my life.

My 20-minute drive to the hospital seemed like a lifetime. A million questions flooded my mind, seemingly racing against time itself. How was I going to tell my family? My friends? What would they say? How long would I live? Would I die a painful death? Would I be alone? Suddenly, time was very dear to me.

By the time I arrived at the hospital, I was obviously shaken up. Crying incessantly, my eyes red and swollen, I could barely see. My trembling hands could hardly wipe the tears from my face. The doctors attempted to calm me down, but they were clearly anxious about me. After some discussion, they decided to run confirmatory tests. The nightmare continued. Two weeks later, the confirmatory tests also came back positive. The doctors notified the Centers for Disease Control (CDC), now also concerned. You see, I was the first healthcare worker to ever test HIV-positive from an on-the-job work exposure.

AIDS, during this era, was a guaranteed death sentence. Most AIDS victims did not survive more than one to two years. People feared AIDS like leprosy. There was speculation, but no one really knew how it was spread.

In anger, I thought, "No, this can't happen to me! I can't handle it! What am I going to do? Not only am I HIV-positive, but now it looks like I'm going to be a media spectacle — the poster child for the CDC." It was more than I could bear.

Reluctantly, I sat down and told my family. Fortunately, they were supportive. Then, after mentally laboring for days, I forced myself to tell my boss. The response was a shock: I was taken off my job. The hospital, fearing the public repercussions, said, "We can't have you, an HIV-positive nurse, taking care of patients. If this gets out, the hospital will be out of business."

Next, I shared the shocking news with my church. To my amazement, some of the members alienated themselves from me. They said, "You know AIDS is God's punishment for gays." Their open prayer request seemed more like a gossip session. I had expected more. I thought the church would be my haven for comfort, solace and empathy.

And then there were my friends. Even some of them became distant. They said they were with me, going to hold my hand. To me it seemed like the handholding was from across the room. I guess they were afraid. I know I was. Thank God for the support I received from my family and a few close friends.

Frankly, though, I was not coping well . . . not well at all. At the time, I had been in graduate school, and in order to function I needed to keep active, both mentally and physically. As I attended class one evening, the professor announced we would watch a film: Living with AIDS. Sitting in my chair, chest tight and head swirling, I watched young people at the prime of their lives wasting away in hospitals. My classmates talked in horror of the disease. Little did they know that I was HIV-positive!

Depressed and despondent, I left class and drove downtown. I didn't know where I was going. I just drove. Somehow, I found myself in the hotel parking lot at the Chattanooga Choo Choo. It started raining. All alone, I sat there in the dark, empty parking lot, rain beating on the roof. I hadn't eaten or slept for days. My mind raced. It raced for hours around a track called "regrets" — regrets on the road called "life" — regrets of never knowing myself. Who was I? I had always been too busy. I regretted not spending more time with my family and friends . . . of not loving, encouraging and supporting those around me more — regrets of not living life. Not enjoying life. Always stressed. Always worrying.

I wished I could turn back the clock of life and push replay. I asked myself, if I had my life to live over again, what would I do? If I just had the chance, I would live my life differently. I knew I would. But for me, that wasn't an option. I was HIV-positive. I had been given my death sentence.

For hours, I sat in my car and stared at the bottle of pills in my hand. I was a nurse. I knew what it took. I determined one thing: I was not going to die the slow, agonizing death of an AIDS victim. I was not going to waste away. I couldn't. I wouldn't! I decided I would take my own life.

I was jolted back into reality with three taps on my car window. It was one of my friends. She said, "Kathy, are you OK?" I despairingly shook my head no. She opened the car door and began to talk with me. She helped me think more rationally.

But the story doesn't end there. Three months later, after having my blood drawn from what appeared to be every vein in my body, I received another phone call. "Kathy, I am not sure how to tell you this or even how to explain this . . . but for some reason all your tests, all eight of your tests, have come back negative. We have no reasonable explanation. Your previous tests were wrong. They were all false positive. You are not HIV-positive."

Dazed, I responded, "Can you please repeat that?"

"Kathy, you are not HIV-positive!" Those six words rang through my head. As I hung up the phone, I had the most incredible sense of relief. I felt like a thousand-pound weight had been taken off my chest. I had thought my life was over . . . and now I had it back.

I had just experienced the worst three months of my entire life. In a sense, however, I was fortunate to have experienced pain, rejection, isolation, depression and suicidal thoughts. They were my teachers, along with the many people — the leaders — I encountered during this experience. Just like the Bees, I had had a choice of whether to agree — or to fly.

I came away from this experience with a new appreciation of life. I had been given a gift — the best gift anyone could have given me: the experience of facing death — and then to be given my life back. As to the regrets — now I would have the chance to make some changes in my life. I thanked God and committed to myself from that day forward: I will not live my life in the same way ever again. I knew if I wanted to be an effective leader and influence people in a positive way, I would have to learn to BEE.

B — Be yourself

E — Encourage others

E — Enjoy life

BEE YOURSELF

Effective leaders value individual uniqueness. They know who they are and where they are going. They also have followers.

Who was I? I didn't know. Most of my life, I had tried to be what I thought everyone else wanted me to be — trying to please others, trying to be accepted. As I was growing up, I always wanted to be someone else. Some days it was Cindy, the homecoming queen. Some days it was Brenda, the valedictorian. Some days it was Pam, the MVP. For some reason, I never wanted to be simply Kathy.

It had taken a crisis in my life to jolt me into realizing I needed to be "myself." One problem: I did not know who I was. I had never spent the time exploring myself. I had always been too busy "doing." Regretfully, I had never taken the opportunity to get to know the one person who was going to be with me for the rest of my life: ME! I made a commitment to spend some time finding out who I was.

Here are a few things that worked for me: My first step was to seek counseling. Scared to death, I knew I had to do it. I had to learn to be. Zig Ziglar once told me you must "be" before you can "do" and "do" before you can "have."

The next step was identifying my purpose, my passion and my mission in life. Then I developed goals. Finally, I decided to set my own guidelines for living.

Kathy's Guidelines for Significant Living

- Filter everything I do through the light of my personal mission: To love myself and to love others.

PRIVATE

- To grow myself and to help others grow
- To enjoy life and glorify God
- Be myself . . . just a little bit better
- Encourage others
- Enjoy Life! Do one "fun" thing everyday
- Eat healthy food 80% of the time
- Exercise 5 days a week
- Maintain my ideal weight
- Journal daily — identifying a lesson learned and one thing for which I'm grateful
- Take off a minimum of two weeks a year
- Read daily
- Commit 15% income to retirement
- Commit 10% income to savings

- Avoid "negative" people
- Spend time with God every day, worship Him weekly
- Always strive to function outside of my "comfort zone"
- Give myself positive affirmations daily
- Focus my energy on changing myself, not others
- Communicate assertively
- Give to others — time and money
- Review my goals on a weekly basis

The last few years have taught me that I function best when I follow my guidelines. I get into trouble when I don't.

Everyone is a unique and creative individual. Be yourself.

ENCOURAGE OTHERS

Effective leaders encourage and inspire others.

I am alive today because a few people encouraged me. Many people through this crisis rejected and alienated themselves from me. We don't have to live very long and life will end up handing us more than a few crises. None of us can control what happens to us. Encouragement and support lighten the burden, not only in crisis, but also in our everyday lives. Here are a few suggestions:

- Expect the best out of people. People have a tendency to live up to what we think of them.

- Offer the gift of presence — not saying or doing, but just being there for someone. Listen.

- Ask people what they need. So often in life we make assumptions about what others need. Ask them. You will be surprised. They will tell you.

- Make people feel important. People have a great need to feel valued, respected and significant. Address people with their names. Imagine everyone you meet is wearing a sign that reads: "MAKE ME FEEL IMPORTANT." Praise people ten times more than you criticize them.

Support the person, process the mistakes and celebrate the victories. A mistake is not a failure if you learn something from it. When someone makes a mistake, support and help him or her process it. What can I learn from this? And what will I do differently next time? Then, when success comes, celebrate! We often do not stop long enough to celebrate our successes. Revel in other people's accomplishments.

I have had the privilege of working at Memorial Hospital in Chattanooga for five years. When I think of encouragement, I think of someone very special at Memorial. Her name is Jessica Branch. We call her Jessie for short. Jessie is a wonderful person. She is everything you would ever imagine in a friend. She is kind, generous, thoughtful, considerate and helpful. Everyone at Memorial loves her. Last year, one of the employee's houses burned down. Everything was destroyed. Jessie rallied everyone together and gave the employee money and clothes to start over.

Then, a few months ago, I was having a rough week. I arrived at work and walked into my office. There on my desk was a vase of flowers. The attached note said, "Just thinking about you. Have a great day. Jessica Branch." In seconds, my spirit was lifted from discouragement to encouragement. This little gift of thoughtfulness made my day!

We also talk about Jessica in orientation for new employees. Last year, we even had a huge birthday party for Jessie. We planted a tree in the courtyard in her honor.

The truth is Jessica Branch is not "someone" at Memorial Hospital; she is "everyone." She is an encouraging spirit that pervades the culture. And although Jessica is not real-life flesh and blood, she is alive and well. It is what makes Memorial Hospital the special place that it is.

When people come to work at Memorial, we ask them to be a Jessica. We ask them to look for opportunities to encourage others. Jessica also has the wonderful attribute of anonymity. Jessie wants no praise. Her only purpose is to encourage. Encouragement. It is one of the most powerful gifts we can give someone.

An interesting phenomenon occurs when you encourage others: The more you encourage others, the more you are encouraged. It has often been said, "Give people what they need, and they will give you what you need." Encouragement: We can't get enough of it.

We all need people who encourage us. Two people who have influenced my life in this way are Katie Bleuer, my mom, who died in 1992, and JoAnn Alexander, my boss, mentor, and dear friend. Who in your life has encouraged you? What did they do to encourage you? Have you taken on the role of an encourager?

ENJOY LIFE

Effective leaders strive to lead a balanced life.

My greatest lesson was to enjoy life. I had never fully appreciated life until I looked death straight in the face. I had always taken life for granted, and I assumed I would live a long, prosperous life. I had assumed I had all the time in the world. Since then, I have learned to enjoy life by:

- Being in the moment. Not replaying the past or worrying about the future, but living in the moment. Ninety percent of what we worry about never happens.

- Living life to the fullest. Balancing work and play. Some of the happiest people in life are the ones who blend the two. I began by making a list of places I wanted to go in my lifetime — things I wanted to do — things I wanted to accomplish.

- Facing fears. Most people's greatest barriers are themselves. I know it was for me. Fearing failure, I had never taken many risks. I found that truly facing my fear and moving through it not only injected me with confidence but also provided me with new opportunities. When fear floods my mind, I try to ask myself, "What is the worst thing that could happen?" Some of my greatest fears have now become my greatest pleasures.

- Spending energy carefully. We have only a finite amount of energy to spend each day. So often, I allowed other people to spend it. But why? I wouldn't allow other people to spend my money. I identified my personal sources of fuel and arranged them into my daily schedule.

Now I have a mechanism to continually replenish my energy supplies.

• Living passionately. Life is unpredictable. None of us knows for sure if we are going to be here tomorrow. All we have is today. Are you doing what you love to do? What are you passionate about? So often, I have heard people say, "just ten more years and I can retire and do what I really love to do." Why wait? I wasted many years of my life doing things I didn't enjoy. I have since discovered the real joy in life comes in living your passion.

There are many things we do not have control over, but we do have control over being ourselves, encouraging others and enjoying life. Because of my traumatic experience, I now know what is important in life. I now know where to focus. I now know, more than ever, that all of us do impact others' lives in some way.

Returning to the Bee family, Hope did not accept that she was "aerodynamically challenged." Thankfully, discouraging thoughts of "you can't fly" did not encumber her. A bee has to be a bee in order to do what only a bee can do. In fact, I'm sure that honey is the natural result of this creature celebrating the sweet success of personal triumph. Effective leadership inspires such expression of uniqueness and enjoys the rewards they bring.

And Nope . . . he began to fly when he looked up and saw HOPE!

The future is yours to BEE!

ABOUT
KATHY B. DEMPSEY

*K*athy Dempsey energizes her audiences through speaking and training. Her creative and unique approach to learning is highly interactive and fun. As Administrative Director of Education and Behavioral Health, she is responsible for leading Memorial Health Care System's (recently named one of the top 100 hospitals in the United States) strategic efforts to become a learning organization.

Kathy is President of The Learning Agenda, a company that helps individuals and organizations discover new opportunities through change. Kathy is a member of the National Speakers Association, the American Society for Training and Development and serves on the board of the Georgia Speakers Association. She is a frequent speaker, trainer and facilitator for meetings, workshops and conferences.

Contact information:
The Learning Agenda
8317 Hamilton Oaks Drive
Chattanooga, TN 37421
☏ (423) 894-8585
e-mail: Kathy@thelearningagenda.com
web: www.thelearningagenda.com

EFFECTIVE LEADERSHIP SKILLS FOR THE 21ST CENTURY

by Bruce S. Wilkinson, CSP

The workplace of the future is constantly changing. Corporate mergers, down-sizing, budget cutbacks, employee/public initiated lawsuits, changing technology and ongoing regulatory compliance issues have forced many organizations and government bodies to rethink the way that they operate. Additionally, supervisors and managers are faced with new challenges in motivating employees while addressing workplace violence, employee/public safety, sexual harassment, disciplining/firing issues and dealing with troubled employees. That is why the managers and supervisors of the future will have to learn how to manage, motivate, inspire and lead by example. They will also have to be held accountable for being consistent with their praise, recognition and discipline when it comes to addressing employee behavior.

Effective Leadership Begins At The Top

Okay, so we know that leadership styles will have to change in the next century, but where will the change come from? It has to come from the top! I'll never forget a conversation that I had ten years ago with a construction superintendent on a 63-story building being constructed under his direct supervision. I was introduced to him by the vice president who told him that I was rewriting their safety and health program. I asked the superintendent what he thought his role should be in this program at the job-site level. He looked at the vice president to see if he would be in trouble, turned to me and said, "When safety is important in the office, then it will be important in the field." That is one of the most honest statements a supervisor has ever said to me in front of an immediate supervisor.

Determining Goals, Philosophy, Culture and Management Style

Managers and supervisors will always react and respond to whatever is important to upper management at any given point in time. Employees will always react and respond to whatever is important to their immediate managers and supervisors on a daily basis, but only if they truly believe that their supervisors will lead by example as well as support them when they perform as instructed. That's why employees will typically do what their leaders do, not what they say. It works the same with parents and children. A parent can tell a teenager to come to a complete stop at each stop sign while driving. However, the young driver will probably make a "rolling stop" (or will "kinda stop") at each corner if that is what parents do when they are driving. Remember, managers and supervisors are the parents and grandparents of the workplace. We all know that managers, supervisors and parents want to be liked by their subordinates and children. But it is better in the long run to be respected by both.

Here's a list of some key questions that should be determined and then implemented by management in order to have effective leadership across the board, as well as employee compliance throughout the organization:

1. What are the mission, vision and/or goals of the organization?

2. What types of strategies, tactics and action plans have been developed by the organization in order to accomplish the end result?

3. What type of continued employment training and education programs have been implemented to assist executives, managers, supevi-

sors, and full-time/part-time employees in understanding this information?

4. What has the organization done to motivate and inspire employees to get them to take ownership in their mission, vision, goals, objectives and philosophy? Are there visible leadership examples for them to follow and model?

Finally, what has management done to convince all employees that it will consistently enforce the organizations stated and documented methods of accomplishing the philosophy, goals, and objectives of their policies, procedures and rules?

Integrating Goals, Philosophy and an Accountability Culture into the Workplace Environment

The next step in maintaining an effective leadership organization is to implement the three P's of establishing an effective culture of responsibility, accountability and understanding. The three P's are:

Well thought-out-policies. Organizational policies are a way to take government laws and and put them into day-to-day workplace operations for compliance purposes. For example, it is against federal and most state laws to have illegal drugs in someone's possession; however, it must be against an organization's policy for employees to have illegal drugs in their possession or body while they are at work. In other words, management (through effective and respected leadership) must utilize implemented policies to determine what type of illegal activity and unacceptable behavior will be considered misconduct at work.

Consistently implemented procedures. Managers and supervisors utilize procedures in order to consistently implement organizational policy on a fair and equitable basis. This usually is accomplished by well-documented training and education programs. I say well-documented because if the manager/supervisor did not write it down, then you probably can't prove that it happened if and when you get to court. The courts will always believe that managers and supervisors receive more training than hourly workers do. Remember, when you get to court, the judge and jury expect management to be the bright ones! In the eyes of a jury, it is usually not considered misconduct if the supervisor knows it is. It is usually considered misconduct only when the employee knew it before doing it. Therefore, documentation of what happened and when it happened is important.

Is there a difference between training and education? You bet! Training tells employees what to do and how to do it; however, education tells employees (and children for the parent-supervisor) why management would like them to do it. In other words, the education element in each training program gives employees the reason for what we ask them to do. It's the buy-in for the employee (or child) that creates ownership! Do you remember when your parents said do this "because I said so and that is all you have to know?" Although we probably promised not to do this to our kids when we grew up, we all got amnesia! Employees react the same way when managers and supervisors tell them to do something instead of telling them why we need them to do it. They flash back to their parents and that's when managers and supervisors start to lose the respect of their employees. It only gets worse from here.

Consistently enforced practices. It is the third P that is most important when it comes to effective leadership because it is our day-to-day visible practices that indicate whether we as leaders will actually "talk the talk" and "walk the walk." Do you remember a time as an employee when you were called into a meeting to be trained on a new program that you knew management would never really implement because of the organization's past track record or history? I'm sure you can still remember one of your co-workers sitting next to you saying, "I'll believe it when I see it." It is our lack of follow through, as demonstrated by our practices, that causes employees to lose respect for us as leaders. Poor and inconsistent practices on the part of managers and supervisors also cause poor morale, decreased productivity, higher turnover and increased employee misconduct. It's true! Most employees are good employees and do not mind fair and consistent discipline for violations of a policy or procedure that they were clearly aware of as either a condition of employment or a condition of continued employment, as long as there has been fair and consistent praise and recognition from management as well. However, what employees do not understand is why they have to follow the rules while others visibly do not. After all, their supervisor said that all employees would be held accountable for their actions. Remember! Without demonstrated accountability from management, there is no respect from employees.

Keep in mind that most managers and leaders get into trouble through their inconsistent disciplinary practices because they forget to implement their disciplinary procedures based on the knowledge that their most valuable employee might violate them. Management usually expects only certain types of employees to violate rules, and they are usually surprised when someone important gets caught doing the same thing! Individual accountability must be part of a responsible workplace, and managers will always be more respected for their consistency when it comes to their day-to-day practices in implementing the organization's policies, procedures and rules. Remember, it's hard to be an effective manager or supervisor if all your employees like you all the time. So you might as well aim for being respected by the majority of employees instead!

Managing, Motivating and Inspiring Employee Behavior

Becoming an effective leader will be more difficult yet more important then ever in the 21st century. Today's and tomorrow's new employees do not and will not trust management as much as their parents did their employers unless that trust is earned. Additionally, workers in this new generation want to be more informed and routinely recognized for their creativity and accomplishments if they are going to be held accountable for following an organization's rules. An excellent example of this culture occurs at Southwest Airlines. Many people leave higher paying jobs each year to go to work for Southwest because of the continuous positive recognition that airline employees receive.

Southwest Airlines creates an enjoyable workplace while still holding employees accountable. Some key leadership elements that will assist today's leaders in managing and motivating today's and tomorrow's employees are as follows:

1. Observe, recognize, reward and/or confront both acceptable and unacceptable employee behavior on a daily basis because behavior is an observable act!

Use one-on-one daily leadership contacts to:
- Motivate individuals
- Give recognition/feedback
- Change attitudes
- Direct behavior
- Influence customer service
- Promote fun/enjoyment at work
- Build respect/loyalty
- Support good work habits
- Change and alter bad work habits
- Determine need for follow-up
- Discipline consistently as necessary

These contacts (as well as retraining or corrective action) should also be documented in a daily log, diary, incident report or to human resources as necessary.

2. Empower employees to take responsibility for their own actions; manage, motivate and inspire personnel on a daily basis and encourage ownership and participation in the workplace decision-making process.

3. Explain why policies, rules, procedures, government regulations and the organization's mission, values, goals and philosophy are necessary without being asked first.

4. Make sure that feedback, specific praise, recognition, coaching, verbal warnings, and reprimands, suspensions and/or discharges are handed out on a fair, equitable and consistent basis. Additionally, there should be no consequences or disciplinary action for performing work as instructed.

5. Treat everyone (employees, customers, suppliers, vendors) with respect and dignity and do not criticize them in front of co-workers, customers and other personnel.

6. Educate employees in how to make the best out of change. Remember:

- Change will lead to choices.
- Change will lead to challenges.
- Change may also lead to opportunity.

Here are some tips that will help leaders and their employees be prepared to make the best out of change:

- Realize that change will come and come often.
- Rely on the past and current strengths that parents, teachers, loved ones, clergy, friends, co-workers and mentors have given you to survive.
- Determine any weaknesses (such as decision-making) you may have and seek help, assistance and education from friends, family, colleagues, seminars or books to improve these areas on a routine basis.
- Create the mind set that with change comes an opportunity for success that may not have existed earlier. Some individuals actually utilize change to their advantage because it forces them to make a decision and take action that for some reason they may not have otherwise decided to do their own.

There are many elements that make up an effective leader. But those managers and supervisors who will be most effective, successful and respected will be the ones who can manage, motivate, communicate, inspire, discipline and document on a fair and consistent basis. But that's not all; an effective leader will also have to make sure that employees have a clear understanding of the organization's vision, mission, values, goals, philosophy and culture. They will also have to know:

- The importance of following the organization's three P's
- Specific job expectations
- Lines of authority/communication
- The difference between clean fun and horseplay/harassment

- How to make specific recommendations to management
- Opportunities for advancement
- Why compliance with written policies, procedures rules and practices is necessary
- The importance of protecting co-workers, customers, clients and the general public from harm
- The importance of realizing where their paycheck comes from
- What type of consistent enforcement will be utilized when it comes to violations of the organization's policies, procedures, work rules, culture and code of conduct
- The importance of complying with local/state/federal, safety, health and employment regulations as a condition of employment

As you can see, it is going to be difficult to be an effective leader in the 21st century. But it will be a little easier if every manager and supervisor realizes that there is not that much difference between being a manager or a parent. Managers and supervisors have always been required by safety/health and worker's compensation laws to "protect employees, from them, in spite of them." In other words, most employees basically have "no fault insurance coverage" when it comes to getting hurt at work. It's also no different with parents who have to "protect their children, from themselves, in spite of themselves." Some children at a certain age think that they have a constitutional right to do what they want to do when they want to do it, and so do some employees. They are both wrong! The United States is not a free country. It is a democratic country with a republican form of government and we all have rules (both at home and at work). The key for leaders is to know how to implement these rules in a way that each employee (or child) has a clear understanding as to why we want them to comply, as well as what the consequences will be if they do not. Just tell the truth!

I always close each of my manager and supervisor training sessions with my P.R.I.D.E. Management Principles for Effective Leadership:

P — The P stands for principles. What are the principles of the organization and can you tell that these principles are alive and well through visible leadership practices?

R — The R stands for respect. Learn to give respect to each employee who consistently follows the policies, procedures and culture of the organization.

I — The I stands for information. Today's managers and supervisors must constantly utilize inspirational and motivational techniques to keep employees informed as to what's expected of them and how they are to conduct themselves at work.

D — The D stands for discipline. Managers must learn to enforce consistently the organizations policies, procedures and rules no matter who violates them. The best leaders can do this effectively and respectfully and still maintain a professional relationship with their employees.

E — The E stands for enthusiasm. Enthusiasm is the unknown force behind success and it becomes contagious throughout the workforce when it is authentic. Employees will usually pick up on the importance of what they have been asked to do when their supervisors are passionate and enthusiastic about their work.

Keep in mind that P.R.I.D.E. Management Principles can work just as effectively for leaders who are parents as well. And remember, both managers and parents want to be liked, but it's better if we just effectively lead so that we can do our job, which is to manage, motivate, inspire, communicate, recognize, coach, mentor, support good habits, teach accountability, change and alter bad habits and consistently discipline as necessary. Finally, a good leader will not coerce or threaten employees to obey policies, procedures and rules, but instead will give them options, choices and consequences and let them choose.

ABOUT
BRUCE S. WILKINSON, CSP

B *ruce Wilkinson, CSP, is a management consultant, motivational keynote speaker, workplace trainer and implementation specialist who reinforces personalized messages with both humor and enthusiasm. He holds degrees in both Safety Engineering and Occupational Safety & Health. Bruce is a member of the Board of Directors of the National Speakers Association and is one of fewer than 400 people world-wide to earn the prestigious Certified Speaking Professional (CSP) designation. Besides his personalized keynote programs, he has developed and presented programs on effective leadership, communication, change, self-motivation, managing and motivating employee behavior, humor at work, customer service, disciplining with dignity, substance abuse, safety and health, violence in the workplace and sexual harassment.*

As president of Workplace Consultants, Inc., a nationally recognized speaking, training and consulting firm, he has presented in 49 states, delivering enthusiastic messages to clients such as AT&T, Hershey's Chocolate, local governments, Lucent Technologies, Sara Lee, Six Flags Theme Parks, U.S. Air Force, various school boards and Xerox.

Contact information:
Workplace Consultants, Inc.
1799 Stumpf Blvd., Bldg. 3, Suite 6B
Gretna, LA 70056
☎ (504) 368-2994
fax (504) 368-0993
e-mail: SpeakPoint@aol.com

Behind-the-Scenes Leadership: What Really Happens Off-Stage

By Jean Houston Shore

One of my earliest leadership exams came when I was a senior in high school, on graduation day. I had served in various officer positions over the years and had been elected Senior Class President. Our senior year had gone quickly and, frankly, our class of more than 500 students was overjoyed to be leaving high school, bound for college, marriage or careers. Since our class was so large, our commencement exercises could not be held on the school campus. Instead, we were to graduate in the brand-new sanctuary of a large local church, complete with balconies and stained glass windows.

The one condition for our use of the church facility was that we were to behave "properly" — no yelling, no profanity and, especially, no throwing of graduation caps (for fear of breaking the expensive stained glass windows.) Well, the graduation ceremonies went quite smoothly and everyone exhibited surprisingly good behavior. My job was to conclude the festivities by leading the graduates in the "turning of the tassel" ceremony. When the time came, I stood at the front and motioned for the graduates, seated behind me in the choir loft area, to stand. They stood. With great concentration, I slowly shifted my tassel from one side to the other, and they turned theirs. Then, with appropriate seventeen-year-old dignity, I walked down the stairs and up the aisle, "leading" my class into the future. I marched more than halfway up the aisle before I realized I was walking down that aisle all alone. Not one member of my class had followed my lead. I looked back and there they were — 500 students throwing their caps in the air!

I did graduate, but I failed my leadership test that day. I did, however, learn a valuable lesson that still serves me well. I saw clearly that leadership is more than holding a title and it's more than performing a role. To be a leader someone must be following you. Even if you're out in front, it doesn't mean you're leading.

As Senior Class President, I was an "out-front leader." The out-front leader should always be positive, should be able to communicate both vision and mission and should persist when lesser leaders give in. We know that. But what many of us miss is the behind-the-scenes aspect of leadership.

Quite frankly, I think off-stage leadership can be a real headache — not the excruciating, debilitating migraine that can put even the strongest of men down, but the irritating, dull, constant headache that you sometimes get behind the eyes. It's the kind of headache you want to take aspirin for, the kind you quickly forget about when something exciting grabs your interest. That's the behind-the-scenes leadership headache. The out-front stuff is heady, exciting, rewarding. It's the part of the job that is glamorous. The behind-the-scenes stuff is difficult, tiring, time-consuming work — rewarding work, yes — but still an undertaking that requires concentration, skill and perseverance. In short — it can give you a headache! However, if you're up to the challenge, if you want to make a difference in the lives of others by making a contribution that counts, if you don't mind putting in some effort to become a better leader of people, read on. You'll find what you need here.

In this chapter, I'll share with you three key lessons about what really has to happen behind the scenes if you want to be a great leader. The things I know to be true about leadership haven't come from books or teachers but through the harsh tutelage of my leadership experiences, both good and bad. People constantly ask me to share with them the things I've learned the hard way. These step-by-step techniques will work, whether your team is a group of volunteers who barely know each other, a comfortable family-like project team or a top executive team looking to make major organizational changes. The expected end result varies in all these settings, but, as leader, your job doesn't. Your role is to do everything possible to give your team the very best chance of success — and then some!

Consider that these behind-the-scenes leadership lessons will be like guiding a group of scouts on a day hike over rough terrain. Obviously there are many tasks you'd perform as the out-front leader of this group. The tasks you would perform behind the scenes would include History Review: Analyzing Group Capabilities, Approach Planning: Drawing a Map for the Current Hike, and Scanning the Horizon to Assess Progress and Danger. Ideally, you will complete the first two steps we'll discuss — History Review and Approach Planning — before the team gets going. These two steps allow you to learn about your task and to figure out the best ways to accomplish it. This is homework — the research you do to give yourself the best chance at succeeding as a leader. If you are currently in a leadership role, you can still go back and complete these steps now. The only problem may be that as you do you may find yourself second-guessing many of the decisions you made before you did your leadership homework.

History Review: Analyzing Group Capabilities

Georg Wilhelm Friedrich Hegel, the German-born philosopher, wrote in 1832, "What experience and history teach is this — that people and governments never have learned anything from history, or acted on principles deduced from it." I prefer a more optimistic viewpoint about whether or not we can learn from history. I say we can learn plenty from history when it comes to leadership — it's just that we don't often pause long enough to view the past with a keen eye.

Like it or not, the collective history of your team is the foundation from which you must begin to lead. You need to know how solid your foundation is. Investigate what history tells you about others who have performed the leadership role you've taken on. Here are some questions to answer:

- What significant interchanges have occurred before in this leadership role?
- How successful have your predecessors in this role been?
- What mistakes did they make and what obstacles did they encounter?
- What can you learn from their experiences?
- How have team members reacted to the person in your role?
- How have those on your team performed in other team experiences and roles? (If this setting is brand-new for team members, this question is especially important.)

You should also take time to examine your own leadership past. You bring to your current experience an abundance of your own opinions and even prejudices about which leadership techniques work and which ones don't; consequently, your current team does not actually start with a "clean slate" as far as your beliefs are concerned. Do some self-examination to determine what preconceptions you bring to the table. That way, you can neutralize their effect on your current judgment and give your current team your very best attention.

Ask yourself:

- What key circumstances brought me into this leadership experience?
- What motivates me to remain in this position? (Note: If you are in a leadership role hoping for recognition and praise, you might want to think again. My experience has shown that the best leaders typically do not take credit for themselves. Instead, praise and recognition are channeled directly to the team members, leaving leaders occasionally appearing to be unnecessary!)
- How will I judge my success as a leader?
- What missteps have I made in previous leadership roles? How will I compensate for these tendencies in this leadership experience?

By taking a look at the past performance of your team members, your predecessors and yourself, you establish a clear understanding of what has brought you to this place. It's like reviewing the successful and less-than-successful hikes of a group of scouts: Reviewing prepares you to know which obstacles the group will surmount easily and which ones will truly present safety hazards. Completing this behind-the-scenes leadership homework will enable you to be a better leader by drawing on the wisdom of the past.

Approach Planning: Drawing Out Your Map

In a perfect world, you would have an unlimited supply of time to spend developing relationships with the people on your team. You would become a detective, uncovering as much as you could about each person and then patiently cultivating the kind of relationship with every team member that would allow that person to be most productive.

In the real world, however, most of us don't have the time (or, if we're honest about it, the interest) to develop that level of relationship with each person. My advice? Choose your battles — but choose them wisely. In other words, find and use a logical, repeatable system to help you focus your relationship-building efforts. Over the years I have developed a simple matrix system that works for me; you may modify my Approach Planning method so that it fits your leadership situation.

Here's the idea: Develop a two-dimensional matrix to clarify your understanding of key characteristics about those you lead. Use this information — privately, of course — to determine just how much time you'll spend cultivating relationships with each person on your team. Plan your strategy for "winning them over," if necessary.

Your matrix will answer three pressing questions:
- Who are these people?
- How important are they to the team's mission?
- In what ways are they like me?

The Six Criteria

I use six criteria when assessing team members as I plan my leadership approach with a new team. I write the team members' names down the left side of the page. Then I create six columns going across the page; these will be labeled with the six criteria. A quick discussion of my criteria follows, though they are presented in no particular order:

Opinion leaders: In every group there are those who can sway team opinion and thus team results. They may be vocal in your presence, or they may influence others more in the background. They may use only past experiences to guide their current opinions, saying things like, "We've never done it that way." They may be logical and matter-of-fact in telling you specific reasons that your approach might not work in this setting, or they may be open to new ideas and concepts. In any case, you'll need to quickly identify the "power brokers" in the group and plan to spend time developing productive relationships with these "players."

Water coolers: Wouldn't it be great if people on work teams used information only for productive, work-related purposes? Unfortunately, leaders everywhere have to deal with people I like to call "water-coolers," though "gossips" might be a more appropriate word. I like the term water-coolers because it indicates the location at which these team members do their best work. These people are usually motivated by the power they think they have by being "in the know." Often, they don't realize how damaging their running commentary on office life can be.

Once you've identified water-coolers, you have three choices:

• Cultivate them as "your" water-coolers, making sure that the message they spread is the message you plant.

• Develop relationships with them, and try to break their immature habits.

• Do not cultivate relationships with them, and keep them out of the real "information loop."

How you handle the water-coolers is your choice, but no matter what your leadership endeavor, it makes sense for you to know where your water-cooler risks lie.

Essential mission: There are those on your team who will require more relationship-building time simply because they are fundamental to the accomplishment of your team's mission or purpose. On your matrix, identify those players who are key to you because of the contribution they must make in order for the team effort to succeed. If a person is essential to the mission's success, you cannot afford not to have that person on your side. Win this person over — no matter what it takes.

Ability to be a self starter: If you read the classified-ads section of the newspaper on almost any weekend, you'll see that most businesses want to hire people who are "self-starters." Unfortunately, many people who describe themselves as "motivated" will actually require regular assistance from you in order to move toward task completion as quickly as needed. Based on your assessment of your team members' track records in this area, you should plan to spend less time with those who are truly self-starters and more time with those who are not.

The next two criteria areas, values match and personality match, evaluate the ways you are similar to or different from those you are leading. In both areas, you want to look at this information not because a particular set of values or personality is good or bad, but because those who are different from you will definitely require more attention from you than those who are similar to you will.

Values match: All of us live by a code of conduct — a set of values and beliefs that guides our actions. Values may include, but are not limited to, respect for other people's property, your definition of fair play and the lengths to which you are willing to go to make a profit. You should spend extra time working to develop appropriate working relationships with anyone on your team whose value system differs significantly from yours. It will take keen observation skills for you to make this determination, and you should use caution in doing so.

Personality match: Here's the good news: You will have an almost immediate rapport (or comfort level) with those whose personalities are similar to yours. The bad news is that you probably do not have a personality match with even half of the people on your team. So, as you assess those you are charged with leading, pay special attention to those members of your team whose personalities differ significantly from yours. Plan to spend more of your time developing working relationships with these people. (Note: We typically run computerized reports called DISC Profiles to help in this step. We also offer this service to our training and consulting clients.)

A recent experience I had leading a group of volunteers showed me again how helpful both the Approach Planning and the History Review steps can be. I was approached by the executive director of a high-profile nonprofit organization and asked to head up an already assembled team of volunteers tasked with pulling together the annual conference and awards banquet. Unfortunately, many of the tasks vital to the endeavor's success were already sadly past due. Before agreeing to the leadership role, I requested information about each of the people on the team — their habits, their track records, their working styles. I also completed computerized behavioral-style profiles on each of the volunteers. At our first meeting I talked openly with them about my expectations, and I asked them to share their thoughts with me. Then I began to prepare my private matrix. I assessed each of the team members against the six criteria mentioned above and, using this information, I planned my approach for developing satisfactory working relationships with each of the team members. To say that this process worked flawlessly would be an overstatement. However, I can say with certainty that our team's ultimate success, at least from a leadership standpoint, would not have been possible had I not carefully allocated my attentions to those parties who, according to the matrix, really needed them.

Remember our analogy to scouting: You are drawing out the map you will use to guide your scouts on their day-hike. By assessing each of your team members against all six criteria and using the answers you find to plan how much time and effort you will devote to developing relationships with each person, your map is completed. The Approach Planning step should be conducted privately by you and should not be shared with anyone. This is behind-the-scenes leadership, after all.

Scanning the Horizon — Resources, Risks, Constraints

When it comes to guiding a group of scouts on a day hike, a leader would need to be constantly on the lookout. Similarly, a leader should always be attentive to three areas when leading a work group toward a particular result — Resources, Risks and Constraints. I call these the dimensions of leadership, indicating that each one is equally important to the team's success, and a focus on one to the exclusion of the other two leads only to trouble.

Resources

Those you lead need the means to be successful at whatever task you've given them. It's up to you to make sure they get the "stuff" they need. Examples of resources your team members may expect you to provide are raw materials, space, up-to-date information, money, clear channels of communication with other departments, personnel and even sufficient time to do the job. In today's rough-and-tumble world, simply obtaining appropriate resources can be a tall order. But it's this behind-the-scenes wheeling and dealing that allows your team to shine. And you, their leader, have the privilege and responsibility of making those resources appear when they should, how they should and where they should. Anyone got a headache yet?

Risks

Several years ago I consulted with an unbelievably hard-working gentleman who was the best I had ever seen in "scanning the horizon for risks." Protecting his sales team from anything that might keep them from being able to sell was his number one priority. If anything — but anything — threatened his team, he quickly took on the fierceness of an enraged mama bear protecting her cubs. His salespeople rewarded their leader with unbelievable loyalty: They regularly went way past the extra mile for him because he protected them so well. You must also constantly be on guard for anything that may pose a risk to the achievement of your team's mission. A word of caution, though: Although you should focus on leading your team to victory, try not to make many enemies. The sales manager protected his team from danger, but he eventually lost his job because he burned too many bridges along the way. Remember, risks come in many forms. All departments of a company are interconnected, so you really can't afford to create enemies, even if you know how to growl loudly.

Constraints

When we think about monitoring both risks and resources, we sometimes begin to fantasize about a better world. We wish for a world where leaders had unlimited power, unlimited budget — perhaps even unlimited control over time and space. Do you think a world with no constraints would make the leader's job easier? It probably would appear to be easier, at first, but in the end we would find ourselves face-to-face with a whole new set of problems. Constraints, limits, boundaries: These are certainly a part of the horizon a leader must scan. You may even be in a situation where the makeup of your team is a constraint you can't change. In the real world, constraints can come about because of time, finances, company policies or a number of other influences. The important thing for us to remember in our leadership role is first, we must understand the constraints under which we operate, and second, we must manage to be successful while still keeping our team safely within prescribed limits.

Just as a troop leader would scan the horizon for dangers and look to the stars to assess progress, a behind-the-scenes leader will constantly monitor the three underlying dimensions of leadership: Resources, Risks and Constraints. In this way, your team will move safely through the rough terrain of the corporate environment, emerging at the end of the day tired and dusty but pleased to have completed a satisfying journey.

The Security Thread

With the improvement of photocopiers and color printers over the last decade, the term "making money" has taken on a whole new meaning. Government agencies continually work to thwart a new generation of digital counterfeiters, and the currency we use to purchase our goods and services has taken on a new look. Many sophisticated devices are incorporated into our newest paper money, including watermarks in the paper and micro-printing in the portraits, visible only under a microscope. One of the easiest ways, however, to identify whether or not one of the new bills is real is to simply hold the bill up to a black light. A tiny, precisely placed security thread will glow under the light, letting you know that the currency you are holding is genuine.

All of us are in leadership today because all of us impact those around us. In leadership, you have a dual role to play: the out-front leader and the behind-the-scenes leader. When it comes to behind-the-scenes leadership, you, too, have a security thread that will be visible under certain conditions. That thread is your integrity — your ability to be true to your personal set of values and beliefs, no matter who is watching. As you conduct your review of history, as you analyze your team members, as you scan the horizon, watchfully monitoring resources, risks and constraints and even as you play the out-front leader, hold tight to that glowing thread of personal honor and integrity. Then, all those you lead — and all those who watch you lead — will know that you, too, are the genuine article.

ABOUT
JEAN HOUSTON SHORE

*J*ean Houston Shore works with organizations that want their people to
work together better and with people who want to achieve more in life.
She is owner of Business Resource Group and co-author of the books,
Reach for the Stars *and* Where There's Change, There's Opportunity!
*Whether she's delivering a keynote on managing change, conducting a
communication skills for managers class, or facilitating at a leadership
retreat, Jean's combination of enthusiasm and expertise makes the experience fun. Jean challenges achievers to new levels of skills. Her consulting
clients repeatedly say that Jean's ability to isolate core issues and her willingness to ask tough questions help them achieve measurable improvements
quickly.*

*Some of her clients include: AT&T, BellSouth, CIBA Vision, Girl
Scouts of America and WORLDSPAN. Jean's best known programs are:
"Personal Bannering," "Leadership and Vision and Making Great Things
Happen." Jean is a CPA and a member of the American Institute of CPAs,
the American Society for Quality, the Georgia Speakers Association and the
National Speakers Association.*

Contact information:
Business Resource Group
408 Vivian Way
Woodstock, GA 30188
(*C*) (770) 924-4436
fax (770) 924-1128
e-mail: Jean@shorecos.com
web: www.shorecos.com

The Secret of Leadership is Preparation

By Rene Godefroy

Anything worthwhile you and I will ever accomplish in our lives is the direct result of how much time we spend preparing ourselves to face the future. That's the major difference between leaders and followers.

When I was living in a poor, tiny village in Haiti, I struggled to survive many deadly diseases. Life appeared to me a long winding desolate corridor with no exit signs. The village was very primitive. We had no running water, electricity nor any access to medical care. According to many statistics, I would never live to be 37 years old.

My mother was a strong and courageous woman — a daring soul. After she gave birth to me, she felt like her situation would not change unless she made a move. About four months after my birth, she packed her bag and ventured to the city — Port-au-Prince. She left me behind with a woman in the village. It was a very painful separation for her. But it was her best option.

Shortly after mother left, I became very sick. Lethal diseases, such as cholera, malnutrition, rickets and constant indigestion, vowed to end my existence. It felt like something was eating me alive. My stomach was always bloated with parasites. I was very frail and weak. When the strong tropical winds blew across the village, I used to hold on to a tree so that I didn't get blown away. Physically I could not go on, but my spirit would not quit.

I wanted to know my mother and father. People told me mother went to the city in hopes of finding a job in order to provide for me. I later found out my father had disappeared. He wasn't from our village. He went around taking advantage of young girls and then abandoning them. I also learned I had a sister and brother living with my mother. I spent many lonely and sleepless nights thinking about the family I did not know.

Some of the people in the village made my life even more miserable. They used to tease me; they used to call me names to belittle me. They'd call me Souyan. I learned later it was the name of a sick and crippled man. Others predicted that I would die early. But they were all wrong because I made it!

As I share my story with audiences, people often tell me that it must be hard to talk about my life. However, it doesn't bother me at all. From those painful moments, I gained some incredible insights. Like a diamond in the rough, I had to endure unbelievable amounts of heat and pressure to become who I am today — to appreciate what most people take for granted. Life taught me a precious lesson: No matter where we start, we can PREPARE ourselves for a great finish.

Leading Requires Lots of Preparation

Most of us have, deep at the center of our hearts, some things we would like to accomplish. But few of us dare to start on the journey. We sit around blaming our circumstances on others, making excuses for our shortsightedness. Then we go to our graves with unfulfilled dreams. Underneath it all, the real reason we don't get the promotion, succeed in the business, or raise a happy, self-confident family is that we fail to prepare. We leave it to chance, hoping somehow things will turn out all right. We float on the ocean of life until we run aground and wreck ourselves.

All leaders have one common denominator: They spend time preparing themselves for the future. On the other hand, most people try to avoid the pain of preparation. They only want something if it's convenient. They go around dabbling with things without any personal commitment. They are looking for a quick fix and something for nothing. Whether it is in our jobs, businesses, or personal lives, being a leader is a relentless pursuit of excellence — mastering our chosen field.

No Excuses: It's Up To You!

In 1983, I left Haiti with a Haitian Theater company to perform in Montreal, Canada. After a few appearances, I escaped from the troupe. Because immigration in Canada had no pity on immigrants, I was facing the threat of going back to Haiti. And that wasn't an option for me, so I paid a truck driver to smuggle me into the United States.

I remember how I had to wedge myself underneath the tractor-trailer between the rear tires in a pushup position. I was covered with dust, smoke and ashes. I had cramps in my legs, and I was shaking. I wanted to give up. But when I remembered my family and my friends back in Haiti who were counting on me for help, I had to hold on.

I had heard many stories about immigrants who had died during the same journey to America. The trip was usually in the middle of the night. The drivers would take off in pairs. The first one would go with just the cargo, and the other with the cargo plus one or two immigrants. When security was really tight on the border, the first driver would alert the second one. Because they had deliveries to make, their jobs were on the line. They would not turn around to go back to Montreal. Some drivers would shoot the immigrants to death and leave their bodies in the bushes to avoid being caught by security.

When I made the decision to go, people tried to discourage me. They meant well, but I was willing to roll the dice and bet all I had on one spin of the wheel just to make it to America — the land I am so grateful for. Because I stepped out of my comfort zone and took the risk, today I am a proud American citizen, enjoying my freedom. I was afraid, but I did exactly what the title of Suzanne Jeffers' book suggests: *Feel the Fear And Do It Anyway.*

I finally made it to what I call the Promised Land — the United

States of America. The truck driver dumped me in Brooklyn, New York. I was excited on one hand and confused on the other. It was as if I were swimming in a sea of change. I had two choices: Swim, or die. My only possessions were one pair of pants, two shirts and five dollars. In addition to that, I was unable to speak English. I knew for sure that life was never going to be the same again.

I later moved to Miami, Florida. Although life had prepared me to face and surmount obstacles, it did not teach me how to fill out an application for a job, nor did it give me any references. I looked for a job everywhere, but for a while no one wanted to hire me. I started out as a boat carpenter; next I washed cars, then painted houses, and mopped floors — for very little pay. Finally, I realized it would require a great deal of preparation to turn my life around.

I share my story with you to impress one thing upon you: No matter where you start in life, you can become a leader the moment you realize that if it's going to be, it's up to you.

To Lead, We Must Build Tomorrow's Dreams Today

After spinning my wheels, trying to make ends meet, I decided that if my life was going to get any better, it would be totally up to me. I wasn't willing to sit around and make excuses for why I couldn't make it in America. No. Too many opportunities were floating around me. I saw too many examples of people who had achieved the impossible by pulling up their own bootstraps.

I found out that virtually everyone in America has access to the same information the so-called "lucky" people have. Life isn't a matter of chance, luck, destiny or good fortune; it's directly related to how much time we spend preparing ourselves. I decided to take control of my life — to be the captain of my soul and the master of my destiny.

First, I needed to learn English. I bought a dictionary and a grammar book. Every day I would write three to four words on my hands, and at the end of the week I would review my words. I paid very close attention to others' speaking patterns. I noticed how they'd make the verbs agree with the nouns. Many times I would pronounce a word wrong, and people would laugh at me. I was embarrassed, but I kept making mistakes until I got it right.

As soon as I was able to understand English, I started reading religiously. I became a bookworm. I read hundreds of books about personal development. Even today, I am like a vacuum cleaner: I am constantly absorbing new information. Soon the quality and the richness of my life began to improve so far beyond my wildest dreams it amazed even me.

It was very easy for me to get a library card, which I used to the max. There is not a combination lock on the door to knowledge with a sign that says "Reserved for the Privileged." We all have the same access. The difference is that some of us take advantage of the opportunities in America, and others take them for granted. Whether it's the libraries, the bookstores or the Internet, no one can stop us from feeding our minds.

Leaders Don't Blame, They Take Responsibility

In order for anything outside of us to change, we have to change. When we get better, things get better. The condition of our lives today is a reflection of who we are inside, or, as I always say in my speeches, the level of our purses rises to meet the level of our minds. Many of us go through life trying to find things and people to blame our circumstances on. We moan and bemoan about how unfair life is, when all we have to do is to be fair with life. I am upheld by the powerful words of the late President John F. Kennedy: "Ask not what your country can do for you, fellow Americans; ask what you can do for your country."

When I decided to become a motivational speaker, I knew I needed a lot of preparation. At first, like anybody else, I had many doubts. There were those who didn't think I had the potential. I went around with a voice in my head talking me out of pursuing the pot of gold at the end of my rainbow.

I joined Toastmasters International. I attended many seminars and bought many books on public speaking. I stayed up late into the night, reading books and surfing the Internet. There were times that I drove twelve hours just to attend a seminar. I later joined the Georgia Speakers Association and never missed a meeting since. One of my biggest goals at that time was to become a member of the National Speakers Association; however, I didn't qualify because I was not making an income as a speaker. With the help of my fellow speakers, I later qualified to become a member. It did not stop there. I continued learning more and more.

The first time I attended a national speakers convention was a major accomplishment. While working as a doorman, I met Dan Burrus, a professional speaker and one of the top futurists in America. He told me a story that hit home for me. He told me to hang in there because when Les Brown, a celebrity speaker, first came to the convention, he borrowed money and rode the bus to attend. Not long after that, Les came back in a Learjet as a keynote speaker for the national speakers convention. I treasured Dan's advice like a diamond!

I did not wait for a break. I stepped out and began to create my own luck. With persistence, preparation and commitment, I began to master the tools of the trade. Many successful speakers opened their hearts and souls to share information and experiences about the speaking business with me. Several have touched my life in a special way. They helped bring the best out of me, even though they didn't know me very well.

Five Ways to Prepare Yourself for Leadership

1. Become an Avid Reader. "Good leaders are good readers" — Jim Rohn

Abraham Lincoln once said that if he were given eight hours to chop down a tree, he would spend six hours sharpening his ax and two hours chopping down the tree. That is one of the true characteristics of a leader. We all should take time to sharpen our axes — read. The average American reads one book a year. What that means to you and me is that if we read one book a month in our field, we will be twelve years ahead of the average person.

The more we learn, the more we earn; the more we know, the more we grow. Think about it: When we buy a book for twenty dollars, we are paying for hundreds of years of knowledge. The price is nothing, compared to what we get from reading the book. For example, Tom Peters spent about forty years of his life studying what makes businesses thrive and survive, even in hard times. He had to study the past masters plus learn from his own experiences. He then wrote a book titled, *In Search of Excellence*, and put the best of his knowledge in it. You and I can diminish our learning curves tremendously just by reading his book.

The late Earl Nightingale in his book *The Strangest Secret* said that if we read for two hours every day on any subject, in five years we would become national experts on that subject. And in ten years we would have the equivalent of a Ph.D. To me, reading quality books is the ultimate joy in life. It rekindles my hope and takes me to new heights. It rejuvenates and gives me a boost. We can no longer make excuses about not having time to read. Today we can buy most books on tape. We can turn our cars into a university on wheels while commuting to and from work.

I received a brilliant piece of advice from a man once: He told me to buy a cheap paperback book, then tear out three to four pages and keep them in my wallet at all times. When I have to wait in line at the bank or anywhere else, I read those pages. Turning waiting time into learning time is so rewarding. You probably have many books and magazines gathering dust on your shelves. You are too busy to take time to sharpen your ax — to feed your mind. It is said that to be a leader, you must be a reader. There is an old saying that, "The person who does not read is not any better than the person who can't read."

2. Network with Other Leaders. In America, there is an association for continuing education in every line of business. If we want to meet the movers and shakers directly, we have to become joiners. It's amazing how accessible the "big dogs" are when we attend the networking events. It's like being a small fish in a big pond. It allows us to bypass the gatekeepers — the assistants — and go to straight to the decision-makers.

The best way to find out which associations you can join is to go to the library and ask for the *Encyclopedia of Associations*. Another great way to network is to join the local Chamber of Commerce. First, however, you must learn how to network and build strong referral systems. There are many books on the subject. One of them is by Harvey Mackay: *Dig Your Well Before You're Thirsty*.

Joining the associations is the best way to sharpen our axes. You'll be surprised how much you can get from building solid relationships with members of your association. It's one of the best methods of preparation. However, we must attend the meetings and volunteer to serve on a committee in some capacity. It's not enough just to be there; we also have to participate.

3. Let Other Leaders Mentor You. Every great athlete, celebrity and business executive can point to a mentor — a coach. They each had people who helped them get where they are. One of the best methods of preparation is to find a mentor — a person who has been there, done that and has gotten the T-shirt — to guide you along the way.

Whether you want to move up in your company or establish a solid business of your own, a mentor can make a significant difference. And you don't necessarily have to have one mentor; you can have many. Over the years, I have gotten some precious advice from my mentors. This may sound simple, but it is powerful! No matter what line of business you are in, you need a coach — someone you talk with about your failures and successes, someone who can advise you. How do you find a mentor? Just ASK!

People normally love to talk about their successes and how they accomplished them. They are eager to help us if we courteously ask them. For many years I failed to put into practice the old advice in the Bible: "Ask and ye shall receive." Don't let that happen to you — ASK!

Always remember the two most powerful words in any language: THANK YOU and PLEASE. Use those two phrases often with your mentors. Send little gifts and thank-you cards to them in order to show

how much you appreciate their investment in you. Occasionally, when you ask someone to be your coach, you might get a no. Don't take it personally; it only means that it may not be the right time. Ask someone else. Don't delay. Look for a mentor NOW! It could be the critical element you need to move to the next level as a leader.

4. Attend Continuing Education Classes. The late Cavett Robert, founder of the National Speakers Association, often used to say, "School is never out for the pros." What a wonderful statement! The experts even tell us that every seven years our knowledge becomes worthless. That means a person who was worth $20,000 as an employee seven years ago is worth probably $5,000 or less today. Here's why:

Our minds are like leaky buckets; what we know is constantly dripping out. I read a story about a man who was working for a company for about twenty years. It seems they always passed over him for promotions. Ironically, he trained new hires who would eventually become his boss. One day he confronted the president of the company about the situation. He told his boss how unfairly he was being treated even though he had had twenty years of experience with the company. The president sat the man down and told him, "No! You only have one year of experience repeated twenty times."

How long have you been in your line of business? Are you getting new knowledge, or are you applying old knowledge? If we are going to thrive and survive in these turbulent times, we must expand our minds. And one of the best ways is to attend adult learning classes at local colleges, universities and technical schools. They are very affordable, and they also have flexible schedules. There are no excuses: IT'S UP TO YOU!

5. Find Time for a Quiet Reflection. The great philosophers, thinkers, scientists, and business gurus always find quiet time to be alone — to ponder, recharge, and flood their minds with images of their future goals. We should never be so busy chasing a dream without being able to visualize it in our minds. There are times when the burdens are heavy, but this is when we need to enter our inner world and examine our lives. Socrates once said to his students, "An unexamined life is not worth living." Quiet reflection is a time to get to know the invisible power that sustains our lives.

Einstein said that imagination is life's coming attraction. When we flood our minds with a clear and vivid picture of what we want, we activate the law of attraction on our behalf. We become living magnets, attracting that which we imagine. Since the subconscious mind doesn't know the difference between facts and imagination, it causes us to behave in a manner that is consistent with our dominant thoughts. Quiet time for reflection should be an essential part of what we do to prepare ourselves for leadership.

A Final Note

I have shared much with you in the last few pages. Please don't stop with my chapter. This book is filled with nuggets of wisdom. Many of the authors are close friends who have shared much with me over the years, so I know their advice is solid. Oliver Wendell Holmes once said: "A mind once stretched by a new idea never regains its original dimension."

In every field, the people who are earning large incomes are the ones who spend time increasing their knowledge base. We need to know more in order to achieve more. We can never solve today's problems with the same thinking that caused them in the first place. You and I need to stretch our minds consistently.

I wish I could meet you personally to find out what you are doing to add value to your life. In the meantime, I encourage you to become a constant and everlasting learner. Read all the books you can, join associations, find a mentor, attend classes, and find time to reflect. Start today! Let every second, minute or hour catch you preparing yourself for the future.

ABOUT
RENE GODEFROY

*R**ene Godefroy is an entrepreneur, author and speaker. President of InsightQuest International, a company dedicated to helping people reach their full potential, Rene's intense desire to learn and his passion for self-development are what distinguish him as a remarkable human being.*

Rene's keynote presentations ignite enthusiasm and a can-do attitude! He holds memberships in the Georgia Speakers Association, the National Speakers Association, Optimist International, the Atlanta Chamber of Commerce, and is a consultant for Junior Achievement.

Contact information:
InsightQuest
3589 Mill Creek Trail
Smyrna, GA 30082
℆ (770) 438-1373
fax (770) 438-1373
e-mail: rene@speakingofsuccess.com
web: www.speakingofsuccess.com

THERE'S A BARNABAS
IN ALL OF US!

by Francis Bologna, CPA

Many of us are familiar with the Judeo Christian story of Saul, the persecutor of the early Christians. He was knocked off his horse by lightning and upon hearing the Lord's voice asking him, "Saul, Saul, why do you persecute me?," he became a convert to Christianity. Saul became Paul, and his writings have survived as part of every Christian Bible. Each day millions of people throughout the world read of St. Paul's life and times through his letters to the emerging Christian churches. Unknown to most of us is the role that a fellow missionary named Barnabas played in Paul's life. Once knowing the effect Barnabas had on his life, one cannot help but wonder if Paul would have been as great a saint had there not been a Barnabas.

Shortly after his conversion Paul found himself alone. It was Barnabas who befriended him, listened to Paul, and believed in him when virtually everyone else rebuked him. Barnabas could sense his genuineness and desperately wanted his fellow Christians to experience the same sincerity. Imagine the sense of outrage the early Christians felt when Barnabas arrived with Paul, the former Christian killer, at their hiding place. For a moment, place yourself in the discourse Barnabas must have had with his fellow Christians as he vouched for Paul. Sense the enormous test of Christian love Barnabas was asking of those in hiding. Isn't it rich with irony that today, at virtually every Christian marriage ceremony, one of the scripture readings is from a letter St. Paul wrote to the church in Corinth speaking of the qualities and attributes of love! There is no question the love he spoke of was founded in the Christ he so dearly loved, and there is no doubt that he experienced that Christlike love from the early Christians who, through Barnabas, opened their arms and embraced him.

As a certified practitioner of public accountancy for almost 30 years, I have had the good fortune of working and consulting with CEOs of closely held businesses and managers of Fortune 500 companies. I have carefully examined the leadership traits of many of these individuals, attempting to discern those attributes that distinguish good leaders from really great ones. A most interesting phenomena! Leadership, as best I can understand it, emanates from two primary power sources: The first, charisma and talent; the second, character and competence.

Charisma- and talent-driven leadership is flashy and casual. In many cases those that practice it, as well as follow it, are politically correct. This type of leader does many of the right things, sometimes unfortunately, for the wrong reasons. The catalyst for this type of leader, political talent, business talent, or whatever the talent, is fueled by charisma and charm. A classic example is William Jefferson Clinton. Our president is talented and charismatic but morally deficient. He practices the will of the polls, with the cost for his success paid at the expense of everyone except himself. He does some things right, as all presidents do, yet many around him have unending questions: Why? What will it cost me? Where's the catch? For despite all the charm, charisma and talent, something is missing . . . character!

Character- and competence-driven leadership springs from a core set of values that people innately understand . . . core values rooted in the natural law, not man's law. Integrity, honor, respect and commitment are but a few of the traits people recognize and appreciate in a character-driven leader. Character is that singular trait that affords one security in the knowledge that a leader will do the right things for the right reasons without regard to personal or financial gain. People recognize that servant-leaders have tested and tempered themselves in the fire of personal integrity. During my early years, my father often shared with his children his philosophy on personal integrity. He would say, "Personal integrity and honor is doing the right thing when no one would know otherwise." We came to appreciate fully what he meant as we grew older and examined, as children often do, not what he said, but rather what he actually did. The catalyst for this type of leadership is founded in competence, fueled unquestionably by character. Given the two modalities of leadership, the most endearing and enduring by far is character and competence.

Barnabas was such a leader. He saw the best in Paul but was blind to the worst. He probably observed Paul carefully before putting everyone potentially at risk. When Paul demonstrated that he was indeed who he said he was, Barnabas' commitment was unconditional. Barnabas was a servant-leader risking his own reputation in the belief of another. Opening doors for others and encouraging them to be their best just as they were destined, is what he was about. Servant-leadership unselfishly places the other first. it treats all with equal dignity and respect. It nurtures within all their seed of greatness, relishes in their triumphs, and is supportive in their calamities. The servant-leader is driven not by personal success, but rather by the joy of the accomplishment of all.

Commitment Culminating in Celebration

Personal commitment and competence are the key ingredients to success. These two keys are important, but unless a third is present, the success is hollow. Servant-leadership is all about inclusion, that pivotal third ingredient in the recipe for success.

Life has a way of teaching us invaluable lessons in the strangest ways. Summer was rapidly approaching with the final day of school less than a week away. It was a great time to be ten. Because my three best friends and I had bikes, we were free to go anywhere in the neighborhood. Our first stop was always the old oak tree in the back of the vacant lot. It was just understood that as soon as we got rid of our books after school we would all meet there. But this particular meeting was to be the beginning of an experience we would never forget for the rest of our lives.

We decided that what we needed that summer was a real meeting place . . . a place we could call our very own, completely free from anything and everything we didn't like, someplace where the four coolest guys in the northern hemisphere could hang out without any hassle. What we needed was . . . a tree house. As we met under the old oak that afternoon, the idea of a tree house began to simmer like a pot of warming milk. In less than an hour, ideas were flying fast and furious as to how we could do it, where, when, how we could get the wood, who had what to contribute. Everything made such perfect sense. The pot of enthusiasm had come to a glorious boil of excitement. Ideas gushed forth from us like milk overheating on a high flame, slowly rising, and then steaming over the lip's edge, spewing down all sides, totally unbridled. We were out of control with anticipation.

Every moment of every day was spoken for until our wooden temple in the sky was completed. If you are a boy of ten, fashion and safety are just words you need to know how to spell for a test; you never really expect to actually understand what they mean. We clearly took a fashion and, certainly, a safety risk with virtually every aspect of our arboreal shrine. Its construction of wood of every thickness defied both physics and gravity. It's a wonder it did not collapse with all of us in it, considering the design did not feature any plank longer than a yard. It towered nine feet above the earth's surface with a presence like none other before it. It stood for everything we could possibly hope for and everything we wanted. It was perfect!

The first official act upon its completion was to post a listing of all those who were denied admittance. No girls, no sisters, no moms (unless with snacks), no little kids, no anybody. We virtually excluded every form of human life except ourselves. The price of that exclusion was that we would spend the rest of the summer protecting, defending, fighting off and worrying about who was going to get into our tree house. The joy was gone!

It took me years to understand the lesson learned from that tree house. And one day, it came to me in a burst! It is in the inclusion of everyone that each of us is made whole. The each of us is never complete until the all of us is included. As a young father of five children, I wondered how much hurt had been felt by those who, many years ago, we ostracized by our little shrine to ourselves. I wondered how my own children would one day feel and deal with the pain of exclusion. I genuinely hoped they would not commit the same foibles of their father, knowing full well some lessons must be personally learned. Sometimes I wondered if there was anything I could do to right the innocent wrongs of a wonderful but foolish youth. The only option was to chalk up the memories as lessons learned the hard way, stored to draw from in a responsible moment.

Tax season has a way of taking its toll on CPAs. So immediately after tax season's end, usually April 16, many of my colleagues and I schedule a day off. Early in April some twenty or so years ago, I decided to take a week off starting on April 16 with one goal in mind. Build a tree house for my children. Drawings were rendered with everyone's input as we labored over the intricate designs sketched with Crayolas on paper from a Big Chief tablet. The children were excited as my wife, Cookie, and I listened and pictured on paper what they dreamed. From time to time we would leave the sketches strewn on the kitchen table to go into the backyard and imagine exactly how it would look in our tree. The word spread like wildfire throughout the neighborhood. "They're going to build a tree house." And there was only one rule — everyone was welcomed! At first this did not meet with the approval of our two older children. Dawn and Pete said, "But Dad, this is our tree house. Why do we have to let anybody else in?"

Why is that we are all that way? Why is it that early in life we gravitate to the more selfish side of our humanity . . . "I have and you don't . . . that's what makes me special." Why are we this way, but worse yet, why do so many of us remain so? The tree house was built and survived long after we moved away many years later. The one rule was honored. Now the children are young adults and as they return home from college and run across many of their early childhood friends, everyone remembers fondly the laughter and good times spent in the tree house of "koo-koo-bombs." Even Heather, who broke her arm for failing to remember you have to hold on to the rope all the way down, reminisces fondly of those wonderful childhood days.

Perhaps, long before his fellow Christians really understood its importance, Barnabas knew the power of inclusion. Perhaps many of the early Christians learned the great joy of inclusion as they practiced it with their former persecutor. Perhaps Barnabas intrinsically understood the real role of a leader is not just to have commitment that energizes, rather it is to have commitment that "synergizes" and culminates in inclusive celebration.

Confidence Born From Competence

Ask any young soldier who has been tested in battle, "Who would you rather follow, the seasoned sergeant or the young lieutenant?" As a veteran of the Vietnam era, there is no question in my mind, nor in the minds of my many military colleagues, experience speaks for itself. In today's business world, employees of many closely held businesses find themselves on the horns of dilemma when the child of an owner is placed in a position of authority simply because he shares the same last name. Parents in this situation would do well to remember that their leadership is born of competence, which cannot be bestowed but must be acquired.

Competence, like any great education, usually comes with an expensive tuition: A tuition paid over time, paid by trial and error, paid by heeding others' advice instead of your own, paid by following your gut instincts. The one common denominator of this education is . . . the price. Many discussions have been had over the years with servant-leaders who spoke of the price they paid, and continue to pay, for competence. Virtually all seem to agree they have some, but the more competent they become, the more appreciative they become of its virtue. When asked of the apparent dichotomy, "You appear so confident and your people trust you implicitly, why is it your sense of lacking doesn't create doubt in the minds of your troops?" Interestingly enough, many responded that their leadership stemmed from a trust among their management team. They stated they have "learned to listen, ask direct questions, research assumptions, not deny the obvious, nor be blinded by greed, honors or riches." The troops understand their leader's modus operandi and know that in the end he will trust in his own good judgement and make his own decisions. Most importantly, the troops know it will be for the good of the whole. The offspring of such a leader are not imbued at birth with such wisdom, they have not garnered the same respect that the parent-owner has earned. They have not paid their tuition of competence.

Manual Gerhardt is a soft-spoken southern gentleman, whose tuition was paid over a lifetime. He began his hydraulic business in his garage some 40 years ago. Today, Gerhardt's is a multi-state operation employing hundreds while serving the hydraulic repair industry. Over the years I have watched and listened to him rally his troops in difficult times when the oil patch was down. During the boon years, he labored over creating opportunities for all those who had served his company well. When asked, "What were the tenets of your leadership skills?" he simply replied, "I guess they know I care. You don't have to be right all the time, but it does help if you are right most of the time. The truth is, our employees know that the decisions we make are genuinely made with the company's best interest in mind. Sometimes, they are hard ones. Sometimes they are decisions of expanded opportunity, but all are made, at least we hope, with the company in mind." Confidence born from competence . . . tempered with care!

Calmness in Chaos

Anyone ever wearing the mantle of leadership for any amount of time has endured varying degrees of chaos. It is the manner in which this chaos is created and endured that endears followers. There is no industry I have had the pleasure of providing consulting services for that is more demanding than the petroleum marketer industry. These companies provide motor fuel to retail outlets at pennies of profit on the gallon. They bear enormous amounts of risk as governmental agencies, such as OSHA, EPA, DEQ, FTA, FTC, to name a few, constantly scrutinize their activities. They entrust million-dollar operations to minimum wage hourly people. The leaders in this industry are found at all levels of management. It's not surprising that when they are asked, "Who do you think has the toughest job of leadership in your company?," many of them honestly answered in similar manner, "not my job, rather my people on the line." However, one reply, "It's easier for me to show you than to tell you," made a lasting impression on me. "Let's take a ride," he said, "and I'll show you the toughest job in our company. She's the person we would most wish our employees to emulate."

It was lunch hour in a small rural town. This convenience store offered gas, convenience products and hot deli meals. The deli manager oversaw the operations. To the untrained eye, it looked pretty routine until the rush began. As I stood with the owner observing the activity, I sensed the pace was quickening. The various bells and beeps of fryers, broilers, registers, dispensers were all clamoring for attention, while customers waited patiently for at least the first 15 seconds after they ordered. What had the makings of a living hell became a symphony as the manager orchestrated her people with the skill of a veteran conductor. She gave priority to items at a pace that was incomprehensible, while serving as a bridge when an extra hand was needed anywhere. The inevitable happened! A young trainee committed an orchestral discord. A basket of hot french fries just out of the fryer crashed to the floor. The owner said, "We'll jump in in a moment, but watch this." His words were hardly uttered when a broom showed up from nowhere and whisked the fries to a safe place. The eyes of the trainee met those of the manager. This was the moment of truth! "Things happen," she said, "Now get a mat to cover the greasy floor, and I'll drop another fry for you." "Ma'am, we'll have your fries out in a moment. May I offer you a small soda, on us, while you wait?"

When the rush subsided, the manager was overheard speaking to the young rookie about the importance of service, but not at the risk of safety. "Your speed will come" she said. "What I want you to do is concentrate on your safety and that of the others. This could have been a lot worse. No harm done. You are sure to be the best fry-guy I have ever had because it took everybody else much longer to make this mistake." As they laughed over the incident, I sensed a bond developing, and I was determined to visit with the young trainee. I later asked the young man, "Tough day! Could have been really bad! What do you think of your boss?" "She's all right," he said. "She could've eaten me out, but we just talked about what caused the problem and what I gotta do." "How did she make you feel?" "Good, I guess . . . I'll tell ya nobody else would have been so cool about it." Would you be willing to work for her? "Sure, she's all right . . . you can tell she's tough . . . but, she's all right, and besides, I'm gettin' the hang of it, and she believes I'll be the best fry-guy she ever had." Applied competence, calmness in chaos, care and concern in the midst of calamity: These are the most endearing traits of leadership at any level.

Courage in Conflict

Some view leadership as an ability to manage numbers and redirect efforts. Actually, that is management, not leadership. However, some choose to practice their leadership in that manner because they are most comfortable with numbers. A number, written on a page, is inanimate — you cannot hurt it, you cannot embarrass it, you can discard it with the flick of an eraser and write another number where the former was, without offending it or the page. Some believe they can lead behind a pencil. Nothing could be further from the truth!

Wouldn't it be wonderful in business if each and every correction of human behavior could be as simple as the whisk of an eraser? Unfortunately, it is not. Leadership requires the ability to be courageous in conflict. When human behavior is inappropriate or damaging to others, a leader must be willing to confront without being confrontational. He or she must be willing to lead by modeling the desired behavior. A commitment to walk the walk is leadership by courage.

Being an effective leader in business is like raising children. Firm but fair! The challenge is to honor the principle that all decisions are made for the good of the whole and not to accommodate personal agendas. As a father of five and an employer of 50, the similarities are uncanny. My vocation as father requires that those entrusted to me mature with a sense of constancy founded in fairness. As an employer, my avocation challenges me to develop those entrusted to me with constancy that creates stability, a fairness that creates respect, and a caring that builds loyalty founded on fundamental principles of integrity and honor.

Servant-leaders are most remembered not for their style, but rather for their character. Their personal character speaks volumes more than their words. They endure because they live their message and live it at the highest level . . . sacrifice. Ghandi, without a sword, accomplished a change in government through personal fasting, proclaiming to everyone but one word . . . non-violence. Mother Teresa cared for a nation and taught a self-indulgent world the dignity of the poor. Her teaching principles were rooted in four popular writers: Matthew, Mark, Luke and John. Her followers were a handful of nuns whose purity of heart and simple acts of unselfish service helped Mother Theresa change the face of India.

This brings us back to Barnabas, the servant-leader who encouraged Paul. He demonstrated his competence in careful discernment before bringing Paul to those in hiding. His calmness in moments of chaos surely won the minds and hearts of those early Christians. His care and concern for Paul were shining examples of his commitment, as the great saint grew in character and depth. Are we not all leaders in some aspect of our lives? Do we all have potential Pauls around us? This world needs servant-leaders willing to sacrifice so that the best in others might be discovered. Are we not all challenged to find the courage to unleash our true potential and accept our innate gift . . . that there is a Barnabas in us all!

ABOUT
FRANCIS BOLOGNA, CPA

*F*rancis Bologna, CPA, has over twenty-five years experience in public accounting and has presented financial management workshops to thousands of owners and managers of independent companies in 30 states. He conducts national surveys of financial results and operating statistics for the convenience store industry and other associations. He is the author of a series of articles on the interpretation and practical application of financial data to improve business operations, cash flow and profitability.

Some of his most requested programs are: "If I'm Making All This Money . . . Where's the Cash?," "What's it Worth? . . . Putting a Price Tag on Your Business," and "Maximizing Minimum Wagers."

Contact information:
Wegmann-Dazet & Co.
111 Veterans Blvd., Suite 1660
Metairie, LA 70005
℡ (504) 837-8844
fax (504) 837-0856
e-mail: FBologna@wegmann-dazet.com

Go the Distance —
the Hole in
the (Berlin) Wall

By Eric deGroot

Have you ever been discouraged in your life?

Have you ever been told that you cannot get something done? Or that you shouldn't even try? That you would not make it? After all, they said, how were you ever going to do it? How could you possibly succeed! If this has happened to you, then read on; I guarantee that I will not only change your outlook but I will change your life forever!

How can I make these claims? Well, this is the true story of what happened to me, and if I can do it, you can do it too! Let's start at the beginning. A journey of a thousand miles starts with the first step. Decide to make that step today, and thereafter do it, implement it and take action!

"I have always wanted to do that" is something we all think or say. Maybe for you it is ballooning, sky diving, flying an airplane, starting your own business, or overcoming your fears somehow. One of my "always wanted to do thats" was running a marathon. That became my goal: The long distance faced by me alone. Could I do it?

Did I have someone in my life who said, "What do you know about marathon running? How are you ever going to finish? You can't go that far. Only crazy people do that!" Yes I did . . . my mother-in-law. It was my dear mother-in-law who asked me all those questions. My answers? Well, I told her I knew nothing about marathon running, at least nothing yet. However, I did know my goal. Do you know yours? Leading speaker Joe Gilliam says "Goals are dreams with deadlines." We all need goals in our lives. Mine was to finish a marathon.

It was spring of 1996 when I decided to run a marathon.

"Only crazy people run a marathon?" Well, I felt very much at home in that category! But how was I going to do it? I must admit I did have some doubts. Maybe my mother-in-law was right — 26.2 miles; that's a quite a distance. I thought of the effort it would take.

Most of us do not make it through the finish line and do not fulfill our heartfelt ambitions and desires. After all, it often seems like too much effort or too difficult even to try. Does not doing it make us feel any better? No, but it is human nature to procrastinate and give in to negatives. If we only realized our true potential and the benefits of trying and succeeding, we could get over the life events and excuses that get in the way. Why don't we? Here are some points of wisdom from the National Speakers Association: We suffer from 1) lack of focus, 2) not being in the know (proper knowledge and training) and 3) too much clutter in our lives. These all applied to me.

Yes, there are lots of loose ends in my life. There are all kinds of projects at home I have been wanting to finish for months or even years! And as an entrepreneur I always see new opportunities even when I am not "in the know." This further dilutes my focus, resulting in too many incomplete projects and more clutter. But focusing on the marathon became paramount. You don't just appear at the start of a foot race of 42,000 steps! I had made up my mind that this was the big one, a real challenge that seemed difficult but doable. After all, I knew what my goal was, and that was a first major step.

I joined the Galloway Training Program, a run/walk marathon system allowing almost every participant to run or walk across that coveted finish line. And believe me, everyone is a winner. To feel that way, you don't need to have the race number with number 1 on it. You don't need to win. Crossing that finish line is what it is all about. How long it takes you is totally insignificant.

Look at Sam Gadless from Florida. He is 91 years old and finished the New York City Marathon in 8:26:00 hours, or Zoe Koplowitz, a member of the Achilles Track Club. She finished the same race in 31:10:10 hours, despite having multiple sclerosis. Does she motivate some people? Does she promote her cause in a way that inspires many people? Her message for me was "there are no roadblocks." We all control our own attitude and destiny. We spend too much time making excuses. What's your excuse for not reaching your finish line?

Believe me, whether you run, walk or crawl past that finish line, you instantly change and find a whole new dimension that opens up in your life. You not only feel you are at a new level, you suddenly realize your potential and those insurmountable mountains instantly become new frontiers to be conquered. It sounds weird, but you want to do it again! Most people who pledge to run or walk just one marathon in their lives are often hooked. Why? The realization that group support, a good system and applying the appropriate discipline lead to a feeling of the ultimate accomplishment. And guess what? That applies to all of us in any walk of life.

My first marathon was October 20, 1996 and I have completed nine within two and a half years. Amazingly, although the distance of every run is the same 26.2 miles, mentally the race seems to get shorter.

In life we call this experience.

You may say, "Well, I don't intend to ever run a marathon." That's okay In reality we're all running in our own marathons, though the tracks may be different. For those of you who are in sales, I will compare running to cold calling. First, in both marathon running and sales a lot of people are working shoulder to shoulder. Second, when you get to the end, there's a big pay off. Third, the more you do it, the easier it gets. However, you know it will never get easy! And last but not least, both adhere to a system and apply discipline. I can say, "I run — I finish" and you can say, "I make cold calls, I get appointments and I close sales!"

Did you know that it takes twelve positives to overcome one negative? And boy, are we surrounded by the latter. That is one of the reasons why I started running, to clear my mind of those negatives. I always wanted to run a long distance race but did not realize all the peripheral advantages. Besides socializing with the members of the group (if you cannot talk to one another you are going too fast), running allows me to be creative and brainstorm about issues I need to solve. Boy, do I have a lot on my mind. Do you? How do you release that anxiety? If you don't like running, fine. But believe me, it definitely helps to exercise, even as little as three times a week. It can change your life!

I signed up and started training. At first we ran three miles, something I had done before. I had completed the famous Peachtree Road Race in Atlanta, a 10K distance (6.2 miles) five times or so. A marathon was four 10K's combined and then some! Every week we would increase our mileage a little, from four miles to five, six, seven, and up to 14 miles. I thought that I could not go any farther. At this point the group proved to make all the difference; the other runners talked me through the distance. Who says that we can or should attempt everything in life alone? All of us in leadership will tell you to have a mentor. Do you have a mentor? Are you surrounding yourself with four or five successful people who believe in you and want you to succeed? I highly recommend you create such a mentor circle as a support group to help you reach your goals and encourage you when you are down and need a push to go the distance. That's why corporations have boards of directors!

The Athens Marathon

After five months of training, I was ready for my first ever marathon. I had signed up for the New York City Marathon in April and would not know until later that year whether I would get in. That made me look at other options. I decided, in that Olympic year, to use my frequent flier miles and run the original marathon race in Greece. The Athens Marathon started at the site where the battle of Marathonnes had taken place and finished in the original 1896 Olympic Stadium in Athens. I would go in the footsteps of Pheiddipides, a Greek soldier, who in 490 B.C. ran the same distance to tell the leaders in Athens of their victory and not to surrender to the Persian fleet, which was waiting in the harbor. His run would have an historic impact on the annals of Greek life. In addition, it had an impact of historic proportions on my life! When I entered the 1896 Athens Stadium, after running and walking for just over four hours, I felt like I had won a gold medal even though the winner had crossed the finish line almost two hours before me! I was a winner in my own right.

The New York City Marathon

As chance would have it, I received a letter from the New York City Marathon organization that I was officially entered in the race in 1996. And that was only two weeks after the Athens race! I was in excellent shape and excited to run the NYC race. Fortunately, I recovered well because they say to give your legs a day of rest for every mile in a marathon, so that meant at least 26 days off. I had only two weeks to overcome the Athens race. The lesson for us all is when you are in shape, rest well and have healthy eating habits, your body and soul are a winning team and able to handle almost anything.

The race starts in Staten Island, winds through five boroughs and ends in Central Park in Manhattan. The energy in New York is always static. You are together with 30,000 other enthusiasts who have all made their minds up to reach the finish line. In addition, there are almost two million supporters on the streets to cheer you on and yell in typical New York fashion — "you guys, you guys can do it." The boroughs are alive with cultural and ethnic differences, but on marathon day the city becomes one big party and celebration. (I heard people saying " If only that one-day marathon spirit and atmosphere could prevail in everyday city life.")

When I got to mile 17, I knew I had made a believer of my mother-in-law, who stood there with a big sign, "GO ERIC," encouraging me to go the distance. "Miracles do happen!" But knowing there were just nine miles to go was no consolation to my aching legs. In reality,

I wasn't even half-way. I hit a wall. In a full marathon 26.2 miles, the half-way point is mile 20. Some even consider it the real starting point. Why? As with any major undertaking in life, as we get close to the finish line we have already covered a lot of distance. We are not as fresh physically or mentally. That's when your mind starts really talking to you — telling you TO QUIT! This is when you need to rely on the right (creative) side of your brain and, most importantly, the fact that you have come prepared to the starting line (of your job, career or personal goal). You have practiced, practiced, practiced, or in this case, trained, trained, trained.

I compare my life now to my marathon running. Over a year ago I was at that wall — mile 18 or 19, and only recently have I crossed that finish line. What walls are you facing today? How many walls have you faced in your life?

There are physical walls and psychological walls. The most important walls are the ones we cannot see. They are those roadblocks that appear in our minds and seem to be insurmountable. Don't forget, whatever wall you have to run through, don't ever compare your weaknesses to others' strengths. The most significant wall for me was also connected to my marathon running career.

More than 50 years ago my parents were on the run in Holland from the German onslaught of WWII. They ran to survive and they ran for freedom. Few people know that in addition to the Holocaust, the systematic killing of six million Jews, over 45 million people lost their lives between 1939 and 1945.

In 1997, I finished the Berlin Marathon, a run that includes the famous Brandenburg Gate, the site of the now-destroyed Berlin Wall.

The Berlin Wall

A short history is in order for those who may have forgotten.

After the surrender of Germany in 1945, Berlin was divided into East and West, communist and free, as was the rest of Germany. Berlin was located inside communist East Germany 200 miles east of the border of West Germany. In the years after WWII, the communist Soviet Union had created an "iron curtain." (A term Winston Churchill had coined to indicate the dominance of the Soviets over most of Eastern Europe). West Berlin was like a small haven in a communist East German country.

In 1961 the Berlin Wall was erected, in effect separating East from West Berlin. The division of Berlin made it a strategic site of extreme magnitude and Berlin became the premier cold war battleground.

On November 9, 1989 the power of the people was finally heard in Berlin, and the wall was literally broken down piece by piece.

The night the Berlin Wall came tumbling down, a new world was dawning. The 60 million people in West Germany (Bundes Republic Deutschland-BRD) and the 20 million people in (former) communist East Germany (Deutsche Demokratische Republic-DDR) were once again reunified and Berlin again became the rightful capital of Germany. (Bonn had served for almost five decades as the capital of West Germany.) Geography remains an important facet of politics in the world. From Moscow to the Atlantic Ocean offshore Holland or Belgium is only 48 hours by tank. God forbid that the Russians would ever have made that move, resulting in us all living under the communist regime. The next time you have a bad day, be glad you did not live in former East Germany where it took 13 to 15 years to get a phone or 18 years to get a car. The hardship that these people faced for so many years should inspire us to make a difference.

Berlin, a city that is close to a millennium old, has a very rich history. In 1788 King Frederick William II, when there was still a monarchy, had the Brandenburger Tor (the Brandenburg Gate) built (finished 1791) and when the Berlin Wall was built in 1961, the Soviets and East Germans used the Brandenburg Gate as part of the wall. Since the wall fell, the Gate has become a powerful symbolic monument for the peace movement.

When I arrived at the Berlin airport in 1997, I met a gentleman from Rhode Island, who turned out to be a physician. His name was Dr. Frank Scheel. We took the same bus to town, found out we were both there for the same reason (the Berlin Marathon) and decided to have some breakfast together. Frank enjoyed the fact that he suddenly had found his own interpreter, as I was able to practice my German language skills on the friendly Fraulein who served our meal. When Frank found out I had arranged a hotel within 300 yards from the finish line and he spotted his hotel on the map miles away, we decided to share the accommodations of this deluxe property. Hey, I was happy to save a couple of Deutsch marks! And what else do you want to do after running 26.2 miles but go to your hotel as quickly as possible and sleep! Because the camaraderie amongst runners is great, we became instant running buddies. All runners are one, big, healthy family.

The day of the race, as always, was exhilarating. The marathon through Berlin was important to me, especially from an emotional point of view. Good meets Bad, and I was there to witness that Good had been victorious.

The race brought all peoples together from East and West. There were 18,000 runners. What an atmosphere! In what was once West Berlin, there is a statue of a woman that cries FRIEDE — PEACE! It is powerful and one of the first historic monuments you see as you run the Berlin Marathon. It is located just outside the Brandenburg Gate, just before you run through . . . The Wall.

The Berlin Wall is fortunately just a memory, but the walls in our minds are alive and well. By running through the Brandenburg Gate, which had become a monument of resilience, hype and hope, I realized that there were no more walls in my life. There may be obstacles, but I now see those as opportunities not problems, as hiccups instead of hurdles or disasters. The Berlin Marathon confirmed that by completing yet another marathon, I was in charge of my own destiny. Training and running have made me healthier and more confident and allowed me to accomplish many things. One thing leads to another. Action is reaction!

Crossing the finish line does not just happen. Nothing in life just happens. The amazing thing is that we all live our lives like icebergs, the top only barely visible and most of our talents buried under water. That is why I challenge you to do what you have always really wanted to do — set that goal. And when you do it, it will change your life too; I guarantee it. Every issue of Runners World, (www.runnersworld.com) includes stories that describe how running has changed people's lives or, in some cases, saved their lives: Whether it was losing weight from 330 lbs to 160 lbs, tackling health issues (asthma, cancer), building self-esteem or dealing with substance abuse (smoking or drinking). A marathon, because of its sheer distance, includes all the elements that help us face and overcome our predicaments, especially those obstacles in our real life that we would choose not to confront. A marathon, however, does not let us get away with anything. We get to find out what we are really made of.

As for me, I have some new goals. I am planning to do The Ironman in Hawaii in 2003, (I'll be 45). A triathlon consists of 2.4 miles of swimming, 112 miles of biking and 26.2 miles of running. I expect to finish in 12 hours. It may sound crazy. But don't forget, finishing is what it is all about.

Applying a strong focus, a good training schedule, a healthy diet and some serious discipline will help me achieve that goal.

We all have our marathons. My marathons have had a major impact on my life. Although most people will not physically run a marathon, I hope that this story will inspire you to run your own marathons, whatever they are, to positive completion.

People are always impressed when I tell them that I am a marathon runner. "Wow, four hours of running, how do you do it?" Strange, by running in Berlin, I realized that my efforts pale compared to the sacrifices of millions of people who have fought for freedom in wars all over the world. And especially pale in comparison to the journey my parents endured during WWII, when they were on the run . . . for four YEARS!

Go your own distance. There are really no roadblocks left. You are free.

ABOUT
ERIC A. DEGROOT

*E*ric A. deGroot is an expert on motivation and international affairs. A multi-lingual speaker and a native of the Netherlands with 15 years of import/export and consulting experience, Eric helps people avoid cultural, lingual and geographic blow-ups. Helping Businesses Grow Internationally: Avoid Global Goof-Ups *is both his mission statement and the title of his next book.*

Eric describes his seminars as packed with practical advice on "surviving the international highways and the country backroads." His clients include: BellSouth, Emory University, Home Depot, Neiman Marcus, Saks Fifth Avenue, Victoria's Secret, and the World of Coca-Cola. Eric is a member of both the Georgia Speakers Association and the National Speakers Association and is actively involved in local community issues.

Contact information:
Exclusively European
P.O. Box 720400
Atlanta, GA 30358-0400
℡ (770) 951-1644
℡ (800) 369-1500
fax (404) 256-5437
e-mail: EadG@att.net
web: www.euroqna.com

LEADERSHIP:
AN EVERYDAY OPPORTUNITY!

by Bob Heavers

There is a leadership crisis in the world we live in today. Whether we inventory world leaders who can inspire millions and literally change the face of the earth or leaders who simply make the moment more precious for those on hand, good leaders are in short supply. We see it in our schools and throughout our universities; we see it in government at virtually every level, in our workplace from top to bottom, in our cities and in our neighborhoods — even in our clergy.

I sometimes wonder if lack of leadership is a result of our fear of failure, or is the price too steep for true leaders to step up? By the end of this chapter you will have met a hero of mine and a story that may change your life forever.

We are living in an age of information overload and constant change, and it's costing us our lives. Consider the price: Are you working longer hours or taking work home regularly? Do you experience the wrong kind of stress? Have the quality and purpose of your work given way to just trying to keep up? Are you neglecting key relationships?

With ever more opportunities to make better and better use of information and emerging technologies, purposeful leadership has been sidelined in favor of whatever is expedient: a quick fix, this quarter's financial report — or whatever makes us happy in the moment. It's often all we can do to just go with the flow and hope for the best. Most of us are too busy to make a meaningful difference, too busy to lead.

We look everywhere but inside ourselves for leaders who are willing to accept responsibility for priorities that are most dear to us. We look for heroes to believe in, someone to rally around; yet we stand ready to blame and criticize at a moment's notice when things are not as good for us as we'd like. Then we start looking again and again, rarely considering ourselves for the task.

I suggest leadership is an inside job. It's about each one of us and the price we are willing to pay to "make a meaningful difference" wherever we go. It's all about taking the gifts we have and multiplying them for a purpose greater than self-interest. The leader we are looking for lives within each of us, and when we call that leader into action, everything in the world becomes a resource to help us bring out the very best in ourselves.

Each one of us has the potential to lead. Unless we presume that God made a mistake in creating us in the first place, we all have a purpose — a reason for living, an opportunity to experience life fully and contribute meaningfully to the world around us.

To the extent that our actions inspire others and add value to the world around us, we make a difference. Leadership has an undeniable impact on others — is sometimes even proclaimed by others — regardless of our title or position in the world. Mother Theresa stands out as a perfect example. Her privilege was to serve. She had no special title, nor did she campaign to be recognized as one of the most prolific leaders in the world. She led by her example, and she did it every day.

The intent of our actions may be little more than moving in a direction of things most important to our own values, yet admiration and respect are bestowed upon us by those who are impacted — changed somehow — enriched and empowered by our example. This is what I call leadership, and it is an every moment opportunity for every one of us.

On the other hand, to the extent our actions diminish others and lead them away from what's really important to them, we can damage or even destroy them. Despite our good intentions, we can make it more and more difficult for others to contribute, pursue their own purposes and live their lives fully.

According to John Powell, in his book *Fully Human, Fully Alive*, in the second century A.D., Saint Irenaeus wrote, "The Glory of God is a human being who is fully alive!" Powell goes on to suggest five essential steps to living life more fully: to accept oneself, to be oneself, to forget oneself in loving, to believe and to belong. These same steps are essential for us to evolve into everyday leaders — willing and able to make a meaningful difference within our own families, in our work environments and among our friends and neighbors.

Everyday leaders accept themselves. They know who they are, what they stand for and what's important to them in every part of their lives. They recognize life as an incredible gift and determine to make the most of every part of it. They find balance in their lives and do not excel in one area at the expense of another.

It's generally accepted around the globe that balance in our lives can be viewed through a common set of personal values. Here I suggest seven areas that together make up the whole of our lives. They give us a framework from which to embrace our lives in their entirety — a framework from which to define success for ourselves:

1. our work or careers
2. our financial concerns
3. our intellectual development
4. our health
5. our social lives
6. our family
7. our spirituality

For the past ten years I've been consumed by a desire to deeply understand the meaning of success. I've asked thousands of clients and special friends, "What does success look like to you?" Some say success is having worthwhile goals and then achieving them. Others say it's giving something back, or making a difference by leaving the world a little better off than when they came into it. To others, success is to be financially independent, or to see their kids succeed, or to learn continuously, or simply to be happy.

Capturing all that I've heard into a single definition has been a challenge, but here it is: Success is little more than moving, at whatever pace one chooses, in the direction of things that are most important to that person. If this definition is valid, the very first step in becoming successful must be to discover: What's really important to me? What do I stand for? What are my values? Only by answering these questions for each area of our lives can we come to know ourselves better and better. It's all about balance.

Schedule an appointment with yourself (an hour to a full day) exclusively to inventory your gifts — who you are and what's really important to you in each area of your life. If you are not sure, keep on until you become perfectly clear about who you are. You might even try explaining yourself to someone you love and trust so you can actually hear yourself reminding you of who you really are.

Once everyday leaders have accepted themselves for who they are, they can be themselves. We can end the charade of acting like we are supposed to act, trying to be someone we are not in an attempt to live up the expectations of others. You see, the clearer we are about who we are, the easier it is to be ourselves. It becomes easier for others to know us and to embrace us for the gifts that are uniquely ours to share. We become more approachable and far more useful to the world around us.

In his book, Powell also says fully alive people are liberated by their self-acceptance to be authentic and real. Only people who have joyfully accepted themselves can take all the risks and responsibilities of being themselves. "I gotta be me!" the song lyrics suggest, but most of us get seduced into wearing masks and playing games. Being ourselves means being free to say "no" when we need to, free to report who we really are and free to pursue what's most important to us. All of a sudden it's easier to make sound decisions we can stand by, easier to find the good in others and in every situation and easier to take action without the regret of negative consequences.

Once we accept ourselves, nothing "just happens" any more. We are undeniably free to throw ourselves willingly into projects and other opportunities to contribute as long as our involvement can make a difference. We sell out to no one, yet stand ready to serve as if service were the hallmark to a successful life.

"SMART" goals help us translate meaningful intentions into performance. Pick a point in the future — maybe a year from now, maybe three. How old will you be? How old will your children be? Your parents? Consider the season of life you are in.

Now reflect on your values and ask yourself a key question for each area of your balance wheel: What, if anything, would I like to see different in that part of my life? In the work part of your life, for example, perhaps you would like to have a different job altogether, or advance in pay or responsibility, or work fewer hours. SMART goals are the stepping stones to success. They move us in the direction of values that are most important to us; so be sure they are Specific, Measurable, Achievable, Relevant and Timely.

Everyday leaders are able to forget themselves in loving others. Once we learn to accept ourselves and to be ourselves, we must master the art of forgetting ourselves in order to love and genuinely care about others. We have to find ourselves in a world that is larger than ourselves in order to experience our capacity to make a difference. Powell says the difference between a "do-gooder" and people who love is the difference between a life that is an onstage performance and a life which is an act of love.

Unconditional love seems the most prized gift in the universe. It's one person putting himself aside long enough to truly experience and to embrace the reality of another, undistracted by his own circumstances or "What's in it for me?" Empathy becomes our privilege. We enter the feeling world of others, and invite them into ours, expanding the world of each other and the prospect of making a difference.

Most of us are drawn to people who love — people who are at

home in the world and seem to drink it all in, only to return it magnified by their joy and enthusiasm. Leaders translate all the goodness they see into language we can understand, giving all of us great reason to be proud, grateful and amazed. They are not blind to distress and the challenges of life. They see struggle as essential to the full experience of life. They are accountable, dealing with setbacks and disappointments pro-actively in order to grow. They choose to learn from their experiences, rather than accept a reality of helplessness, recurring mistakes and despair.

Leaders who love easily see the good in others, celebrate and encourage them and are there for them. Their commitment to love makes them willing servants of others, accountable and free to extend a helping hand without concern for their own needs — like the Biblical reference to Jesus saying, "The greatest among you will be the servant of all." They put personal inconvenience aside to experience life as an incredible gift only to be shared with others. They are practicing disciples of a law shared with me as a young man — it may well be the law of the universe: Whatever one gives, unconditionally and with no strings attached, will come back in equal or greater proportion. Choose to magnify life and the goodness in others by loving unselfishly.

Everyday leaders find reason to believe in something much larger than themselves. Having discovered the magic of putting themselves aside for others, they are free to discover meaning in life — a person or a cause to which they can rededicate their lives. This commitment shapes their lives and makes all their efforts seem purposeful and worthwhile.

To believe requires faith — faith in what the future can be, faith in the difference one's life might make for another, faith that good will always come from good intentions put into action. Good leaders are dreamers of sorts who develop the habit of looking beyond themselves to "what could be." They are committed, and their confidence empowers us to consider grander visions and possibilities for our own lives.

True leaders are willing to believe in possibilities, and they have mastered the art of "letting go" rather than taking control. They relinquish control in order to gain personal power — power over themselves. They admit their own limitations and are free to focus on the needs of others. They are filled with awe and appreciation for the world around them and those who cross their paths. Their lives become irreversibly dedicated to the potential of those around them.

Everyday leaders find meaning in life that goes beyond the satisfaction of self. They live in a world full of needs to be met. They realize their own capacity for making a difference and stay committed to helping others bring out the very best in themselves as well. They believe in vision yet are courageous enough to recognize their own weaknesses. Ironically, they become weak enough to serve, strong only in their faith that life is a gift that deserves to be lived to the fullest by every one of us. Their lives are testimonies that change the lives of others for the better — forever.

The final prerequisite to good leadership is to belong. Fully alive people are at home wherever they go because they know themselves and others well enough to realize how much we have in common. They belong to others, and others belong to them. They would be missed, just as they are remembered, were they not present.

They are willing to share the very best in themselves and to anticipate the very best from others.

Everyday leaders shun sameness; rather they yearn for the harmony of our differences. They are eager to hear different points of view and seem never to tire of dreams and visions of "what could be." Because they believe, they are free to explore new possibilities and to share their own vision in a way that others can understand. Rather than stand alone, they participate as one of the team. They empower other team members and never lose sight of the dream.

Everyday leaders have little need to separate themselves from others. Their power comes not from standing alone but from attracting contribution and partnership from others. Harnessed to others of like purpose, they find great satisfaction in both giving and receiving. It's all for one and one for all — always room, always time for one more. The organization, the team, the family, the church, the event, the company, the transaction — everything is better because this person belongs.

What a wonderful place this would be if everyone would decide to belong to each other! Caring would become effortless and lives would be enriched as we stood up to be counted upon for support and encouragement, like one couple stepping onto the dance floor not just to enjoy each other but also to make it much easier for others to join in the dance.

Which brings me to my hero. Meet "Clarence." Clarence is a fictional character who first came to life at our supper table nearly ten years ago. Amy, my oldest child, was in ninth grade and decided to run for president of her brand-new high school.

She, along with other candidates, would have to stand in the center of a packed gym and let all the other students know why she'd like to be elected president. She was not one of the more popular kids in the school, not known well by others — but she had purpose and the determination to make a difference. Amy believed that every student — not just the athletes, cheerleaders and more popular kids — should get a chance to participate more fully in school activities.

Clarence was a senior and still a bit of a nerd. He showed up at nearly every game and special event throughout his high school career, but he never participated and was never welcomed by others. He would hang out with a handful of other misfits, always at arm's length from the action, expecting to take abuse if he tried to get even remotely close to the "cool" kids.

The spring dance would be the last school event of his career, and Clarence didn't want to end his high school career sitting on the bench with the rest of his kind, watching all the cool kids play. He wanted to dance. When he told his buddies he was going to dance, they rolled in laughter but promised to be on hand for the spectacle.

As Clarence approached the gym, he could hear the music, and he knew what he had to do. As he entered the gym his classmates could hardly believe it. Clarence was the only kid at the dance wearing a tie. He was wearing a suit that must have fit him a few years back, shiny black shoes and white socks that could be seen below his shin-high dress pants.

Even his fellow nerds made fun of him and the way he was dressed. Nevertheless, he assured them that tonight he was going to dance. Each time Clarence got up, his buddies would get ready for the big shutdown. He'd head for the other side of the gym, where all the wallflowers were seated, then lose his nerve near the punch bowl located on a table midway across the gym floor.

After the band's last break of the night, Clarence knew this would be his last chance. He headed straight for the punch bowl, hesitated for just a moment, then made a beeline for the girls' side of the room. His buddies were beside themselves, and by the time Clarence had been rejected by each of the first five girls that he asked, his buddies were nearly hysterical with laughter. In fact, they caused such a commotion that everyone on the dance floor looked to see what was going on. They, too, got a good laugh, and when they all stopped dancing to watch, the band stopped playing.

The scene was pathetic. Soon the room grew so silent you could have heard a pin drop. There was Clarence. "Would you dance with me?"

"No, Clarence, never with you." And he went to the next girl.

"Would you dance with me?"

"No, Clarence, get away from me. You are embarrassing me."

Then to the next, "Would you dance with me?"

Finally, just when everyone in the gym was feeling his pain, the cute young girl seated in front of him looked up at Clarence and said, "I'd love to dance with you."

As the two of them stepped onto the dance floor, the crowd parted, making a path for them to the center of the dance floor. Then Clarence looked up at the band as if to say, "Where's the music?" As the band started to play, everyone now surrounding them stood by in awe of what just happened. As Clarence and his partner started to dance, none too gracefully, everyone else on the dance floor and everyone now standing along the sides of the gym began to applaud — sustained, generous and very emotional applause. Within minutes, everyone joined in the dance — the dance they would always remember. All the wallflowers from both sides of the gym joined in the dance, too, leaving behind only a legacy of "how they used to be."

Clarence is not my only hero. The day Amy delivered this story to a packed gymnasium, I could hardly stay away. Parked along the wall, near the bleachers at the far end of the gym, Amy's grandmother and I didn't miss a word of it. Through tears of immense pride I said to myself, "Thank you, Amy! I love you and am so proud to be your dad. Thanks to your courage, my life has been enriched forever. You will always be very important to me, and your story will be shared with many, many others."

And so I share this story with you. Amy wasn't elected president, but she left an indelible challenge with every student and faculty member who heard her message. That day Amy was a leader, and the difference she made absolutely added value to everyone fortunate enough to recognize the gift of leadership she had just shared.

ABOUT
BOB HEAVERS

*B*ob Heavers is dedicated to helping people and organizations bring out the very best in themselves. He owns the Denver franchise for Priority Management International, an independent, entrepreneurial training network committed to improving performance worldwide. Through public workshops, tailored retreats and customized training programs, Bob and his organization help busy people learn to manage their personal and professional lives more fruitfully without feeling overwhelmed.

Bob's background includes years of general management experience with healthy, as well as troubled companies. He has a remarkable grasp of values driven leadership and a knack for getting people to rededicate themselves to shared goals. Losing his spouse to cancer fourteen years ago, Bob has learned to turn adversity to opportunity and knows how tough it can be to juggle a busy life. He's grown a very successful business while, as a single parent, raising three great kids.

Contact information:
Heavers & Associates, Inc.
16278 East Crestline Lane
Aurora, CO 80015
℘ (800) 368-4831
℘ (303) 680-5015
fax (303) 680-5223
e-mail: Heavers@aol.com

MAKE A DIFFERENCE BY KEEPING COMMITMENT, FLEXIBILITY AND PERSEVERANCE ON YOUR TEAM

By Deborah L. Dahm

I believe most of us are good leaders, yet as I grow older — and hopefully wiser — I ask myself if being a good leader is enough? At least for me, the answer is no. I have had the opportunity and good fortune to work and live with some extraordinary leaders who have taught me much. What did those leaders have in common? What qualities did they share? What stands out is that each one of these extraordinary leaders had a vision that incorporated commitment, flexibility and perseverance.

As a youngster I grew up near a lake. My father's hobby was sailing, and he often sailed in competitions. I still remember the two of us preparing for the starting gun to blow, always keeping our eyes on the finish line, with such hope of winning a trophy.

When I first started sailing as a very young child, it was hard for me to comprehend my father suddenly saying, "Deborah we're going to tack in a few moments."

I would protest, "But Dad, the finish line is straight ahead. Why would we go over there?" and point to another direction. Dad would explain how the wind had shifted, and that in order to reach the finish line we must follow the wind, trust and be flexible. To my childlike amazement we would sail through the finish line — often first! My eyes would focus back to the other boats that had chosen not to change directions and were in the water, going nowhere. As I look back on those wonderful learning experiences, I am reminded that much of life is like a sailboat race.

Besides being a wonderful sailor, my father was also an innovative, insightful and successful entrepreneur who owned a construction company. Dad built beautiful, exciting, high-quality custom homes and professional buildings. He always crafted and implemented his designs with a vision of what the future held and what his clients wanted. He had the foresight and the flexibility to see the changing economics with rapidly increasing costs of electricity and materials. He knew that he had to be open and flexible to further change. Wanting to continue to provide the quality that was his hallmark, my father began designing and developing some of the most efficiently built earth shelter homes. When you stand in front of an earth shelter home, it looks like a regular house with a traditional roofline. But these homes are built into the earth, with huge windows across the front of the house that allow the sun to aid in the heating of the home, creating an extremely energy-efficient dwelling.

Dad's ability to be flexible — to tack — not only facilitated his business to flourish, but also helped his clients have the homes of their dreams, homes they could comfortably afford and maintain.

I, too, had a dream: a vision of becoming a professional speaker and author.

That's when I started my own enterprise: Accredited Seminars & Presentations. Beginning with a plan in mind — at least I thought I had a plan — in reality, my career has taken many shifts and changes in direction. Some doors have closed that I believed would always be open, yet new doors have opened, presenting me with even greater opportunities.

How many times in our lives do our plans and goals shift direction? To accommodate the shifts, we must take risks into unknown territory, not remain attached to the final destination. There will always be risk in life. I remember that those times my Dad would tack too soon or too late, the other boats would sail by, but when my father would trust his own instinct and risk to win, he almost always finished on top.

To enjoy fulfilling lives we need to be open to those changes that life's compass gives us, risking and ultimately trusting our own intuition:

- Listen and trust your inner thoughts and instincts.
- 60/30: read 60 minutes a day and of 30% of what you read, read outside of your area of expertise, looking for trends and changes.
- Listen to the needs, desires and insights of the people whom you lead as well as to those of people you consider your mentors.

We've all heard the saying, A penny for your thoughts. But have you ever heard, a penny per pinecone? What a penny per pinecone means to me is perseverance.

Imagine, during the last years of the Depression era, a preschool-aged child with blond, curly hair picking up pinecones in her grandparents' farmyard in rural Kansas. She places them so delicately in her treasure sack, hoping to sell them to nearby neighbors for a penny per pinecone. Wanda Lou is her name. Now, keep in mind that the neighbors all have hundreds of pinecones in their own yards, and these neighbors' yards are not side by side, but separated by tens of acres. As far as Wanda Lou is concerned, these are not obstacles.

Now imagine two parents, frantic from searching for their young daughter, watching Wanda Lou return to the yard, her face smiling and full of excitement and pride as she holds up her paper bag. Her father looks down at Wanda Lou, his blue eyes piercing as she opens her bag to reveal dozens of pennies.

"Where did you get these pennies, Wanda Lou?" he asks.

Innocently she replies, "I got pennies per pinecone."

Her father remains silent as he gazes around his yard at the hundreds of pinecones, appreciating there are just as many in everyone else's yards. He realizes Wanda must have walked miles to sell that many pinecones to people who quite frankly did not have a penny to spare.

Quiet pride is what he felt, for Wanda's father recognized that same type of perseverance within himself: a man who set off to the big city day after day to sell life insurance during the middle of the Depression. This man had become a true legend in his profession, honored as a member of the million-dollar round table for several decades and recipient of the greatest of all honors in that industry — a place in the Insurance Hall of Fame.

Perseverance: It's all in how you look at life — your attitude. Do you see a problem as an obstacle or do you see that same problem as an opportunity and an adventure towards growth for you and the people you lead?

Wanda Lou is my mother. I learned much from both her and my grandfather. I learned the legacy of perseverance from my grandfather, Charlie, an insurance salesman, and my mother, Wanda Lou, who would always say, "You can do it!" and "The glass is always half-full."

During my sophomore year of high school, I was in a severe car wreck. I endured not only a severely fractured right ankle but torn and dislocated ligaments as well. I lay in the hospital for many days, having had five surgeries, with the left side of my face becoming more and more numb and an ankle that was rapidly becoming grossly infected. What I particularly remember, though, is the fun that I had with all the wonderful attention from my high school friends, the great cards, flowers and gifts.

My biggest concern at that particular moment in time was making it to the last basketball game of the season. When the doctor came to see me, I remember looking up him, feeling a little fragile and in a great deal of pain. I told him, "Dr. Ice, I am a cheerleader, and we have our last basketball game in 15 days and I am planning on being there." I was smiling. What could he say?

The fourteenth day of my hospital stay came after many ups and downs. My ankle became infected, which meant surgery would have to be postponed.

Eventually the left side of my face was completely numb. There were days I didn't have the energy to do anything but lie there.

Finally, on the evening of the 14th day, Dr. Ice walked into my room, where my parents were sitting among the flowers, candy and gifts that reflected only thoughts of optimism. He turned to face me and said, "Deborah, your fever has been down for a couple of days; the surgeries were successful, so you may go home tomorrow morning."

Tears of joy filled my darkened eyes; at the same time, I couldn't stop smiling from ear to ear. Turning to my parents, I said, "Get the car packed now! I'm not going to sleep here one more night. I'm going to go home now!" I did.

Two weeks later I saw Dr. Ice for the first time since my hospital dismissal. The first thing he asked was, "How was the game, and who won?" I beamed with excitement and pride. I told him it had been great to be there to cheer with my friends who had been there for me these past couple of weeks. I couldn't tell him who had won though, as my father and mother had taken me home soon after the halftime because I was still tired and weak from the accident. I suspected he already knew, or that it really didn't matter to him. He had come to know a young girl of sixteen who'd had the perseverance to survive and was determined to see the world as positively as possible. That's what obviously mattered to him.

Actions to take when faced with an obstacle/opportunity:

1. Step back a day or so to get some distance between you and the problem.

2. Never make a decision when you're in an emotional state.

3. Talk with the people you lead to keep them in the know, allowing them to brainstorm ideas.

Booker T. Washington said, "Success is to be measured not so much by the position that one has reached in life but by the obstacles one has overcome while trying to succeed."

Extraordinary leaders are people who are committed not only to seeing themselves successful, but also to helping the people they lead be the best they can be. These are leaders who also realize leadership doesn't happen overnight. They have the ability to learn and grow, constantly checking in with themselves and being willing to practice, practice, practice.

When I think about commitment and regular practice I am reminded about my own daughter, Katie, who is 15 years of age. Not long ago I took her to be fitted for her first pair of pointe shoes. This event was the culmination of her nine years of ballet practice twice a week, month after month. Now, many of us may think, What's the big deal? Like me, you may be thinking, "This fitting should only take a few moments." However, as the owner of this highly specialized store looked at her foot and sized it, I realized that this was not going to be a quick shopping event but one that might last several hours. It did. Katie tried on dozens of hand-crafted pointe shoes, one after another, getting closer and closer to finding the right fit, committed to making this special event rewarding.

As I watched Katie's face, I saw her become fatigued and her feet become raw, as all new pointe dancers' feet do. Not once, though, did Katie complain of her sore toes. This step was part of the process, and she was completely committed to her art and to enjoying it.

Committed leaders not only help themselves and others succeed; they also listen carefully, educate themselves and others and make others part of the decision-making process. Thus, they help others take ownership of their actions and celebrate even the smallest of successes.

Recently Katie's best friend broke up with her boyfriend, a painful time in any teenager's life. As Katie listened to her friend, she calmly began to share her own insights. Katie asked her friend to try to look at the bigger picture, helping her to see the opportunity in front of her. Katie asked her friend to list her strengths. Her friend continued to weep, but this time in realization that some of the choices ahead of her were good.

Katie did not try to take on her friend's problem. She gave insights, allowing her friend to find her own answers. Leaders need to allow people to discover their own insights, helping them to take ownership of their behavior.

When we take time to listen to people, trying to see another point of view and perspective, people feel honored for who they are. Keep in mind that listening is an active process, one in which we must inject our intensity into the conversation, even if we don't say a word. Listening is not only using our eyes and ears but also opening our hearts.

When you're committed, you want to make sure the people you lead are correctly educated to accomplish what's most important to them. Once you assess the educational needs of your team, ask and involve them in how they will accomplish this goal. When they believe their opinions and ideas are important to you, they will be more willing to share and take risks with their ideas and will feel more empowered. Don't quit there, though. As they accomplish each step toward that commitment, celebrate! Studies show the number-one reason people follow great leaders and stay with an organization is they feel appreciated and respected for who they are.

When I became the education nurse for a surgical and recovery department of a hospital, one of the requirements was to get a certification called CNOR. Terry Voight, my supervisor, whom I still remember vividly because of his extraordinary ability to lead, asked me what I needed from the department to achieve this goal. I was able to share my ideas of what I needed, realizing not only was my opinion important, but also I was important to the department as a person. After six months of studying and generous support from the department and Terry, the daylong exam finally came. Six weeks later I found out I passed with flying colors, and believe me, I wasn't the only one who celebrated! Terry gave us a department celebration.

Commitment to Others:

- Listen authentically.
- Educate yourself and others.
- Make them part of the decision-making process.
- Celebrate!

As President of the National Speakers Association of Kansas City, it's so important for me to not only help the people I lead to grow and empower themselves but to also empower and nurture my own growth. What I have done for myself this year to keep growing in leadership is to educate myself. When I walk into a bookstore, I am overwhelmed at the number of books and magazines there are to choose from. When I speak with an audience, I enjoy sharing new books that I have found and asking the audience to share with me new books they have read. I am constantly looking for books and magazines that give me new insights, ideas and mindsets to synchronize with my own ideas. Once I discover those ideas, I write down these new insights and how they apply to me and my own unique situations and style.

To be an extraordinary leader, I have been told time and time again to surround myself with those people whom I want to emulate and who seem to continually reach beyond their own greatness to mentor others. Having mentors has been an important part of my personal commitment. These people are open to sharing their ideas and strengths, encouraging me to see life from a different perspective. As I learn from them, I, in turn, try to mentor others.

Commitment to Self:

- Read magazine articles and books on leadership daily.
- Find great mentors and people for you to mentor.
- Listen to the needs of the people you lead.

Every one of these individuals about whom I have written exemplifies what it means to be an extraordinary leader who makes a lasting impact on others' lives. The characteristics of perseverance, flexibility and commitment remain important aspects in my life that I try to improve daily. These qualities continue to help me through whatever stage in life I may find myself.

For example, not long ago I was diagnosed with lupus as well as fibromyalgia, a muscle syndrome. I'll never forget the day when the physicians informed me of the ramifications of these two diagnoses, just as I was heading out for a five-day National Speakers' Convention. The progression of these diseases would mean chronic fatigue, muscle weakness and joint pain. I was faced with the possibility of having to end my traveling career, which I love passionately.

As I looked out the airplane window heading towards the national convention, I asked myself, "What am I going to do if all these predictions come to fruition?" I silently started laughing, thinking about the profession I was in. Being a trainer, a consultant, a keynoter, speaker, and an author isn't the easiest profession in the best of times, but now I was more than a little afraid for my future. Immediately retreating within myself, I remembered the lessons that I had learned along the way from my parents, my daughter and the many supervisors and managers whom I had met along the way. The flexibility that my father and his sailing taught me reminded me I needed to start planning different options, alternatives and "tacking strategies" with the possibility of this new life direction.

The perseverance that my mother inspired in me reminded me I would get through anything that God placed in my path as long as I had a purpose in life.

At that moment, 30,000 feet in the air, my purpose was never so clear: to share my thoughts, ideas and passion with the people I work with and to always give words of encouragement.

As for commitment, there are days when I find myself in a great deal of pain, stiff and unable to walk without the help of a cane. Yet, I remember the lesson my daughter consistently taught me through her hard work in her art. And for me, too, the show must go on.

Are these qualities that you have within your repertoire? Are these qualities that you believe and feel to be significant if you are a supervisor, manager or the boss? Remember to find the resilience to be flexible and tack with life changes, the perseverance to meet any obstacle you may come across, and the commitment to practice, practice, practice.

ABOUT
DEBORAH DAHM

*D*eborah Dahm is known as the Speaker that Listens. She is an internationally respected trainer, consultant, educator and author with 20 years experience. She has worked with corporations and associations — helping thousands to maximize their effectiveness in leadership, communication and management of time and relationships. Her goal is to always leave a lasting impact so people are able to achieve their most important goals and leave their lasting legacy.

Deborah is president of Accredited Seminars & Presentations and the author of Time Management through the Enneagram, *which deals with management of time based on personality. Deborah brings valuable information, light-hearted enthusiasm and compassionate candor that will lead you and your employees to new levels of effectiveness. Her warm and sincere presentation style will inspire each of you to develop a proactive and positive approach to your life. She is a member of the National Speakers Association and President of the Kansas City Chapter.*

Contact information:
Accredited Seminars & Presentations
3315B Covington Court
Hutchinson, KS 67502
℘ (316) 663-3371
fax (316) 663-3372
e-mail: dldahm@midusa.net
web: www.deblistens.com

SECRETS FOR MOTIVATING OTHERS TO DO WHAT YOU WANT

by Doug Smart, CSP

Here's a principle of leadership that will help you bring out the best in others: everyone is motivated. And for effective leadership, that's good news. As a leader you can rely on this principle to get virtually anything accomplished. Oh, a person may not be motivated to do what you want or to do it when you want it (my teenage son comes to mind and the angst he expresses over his chores of emptying the dishwasher and mowing the lawn), but each person holds certain "motivators" that appeal to a personal sense of comfort. Comfort, in this case, is not about lounging, laziness or being pampered; based on the individual's personality style, everyone — even teenagers, co-workers and customers — has comfort triggers that can cause positive responses (motivators) or negative responses (de-motivators). Recognizing these comfort triggers will make it easier for you to motivate others to do what needs to be done.

Directiveness and Affiliativeness

Spotting and understanding motivators and de-motivators are based on two traits we all share in common. One trait is our "directiveness." Some have a strong need to direct what is happening around them. They enjoy telling other people what to do and how to do it, and they are assertive. For example, this could be the person who regularly volunteers to chair committees, frequently voices opinions, and finds decision making exciting. At the opposite end are people who are comfortable following the lead of others. They take direction well, don't feel it is necessary to stand out in order to be effective, and are uneasy making definitive decisions. They often defer to others.

Actually, when it comes to directiveness, each of us moves up and down the directiveness scale depending on the events. For example, in a tense moment, such as perceiving that someone might be a threat to your children, your gut reaction is to zoom instantly to a super-direct position and bark: "Get away from them! Leave my family alone!" You suddenly epitomize the top of the scale. Conversely, there are situations in which you readily become submissive, such as when you are stopped for speeding, you realize you can't avoid the ticket, and your mild-mannered side responds with a meek, "Yes, officer." Through the years you have come to favor one of four stages of directiveness: very direct, mildly direct, mildly deferential and very deferential. You live in one of the four stages more than the other three.

The second trait we all share in common is our "affiliativeness." Some people have a strong need to be around other people. They relate well to the feelings and needs of others and are particularly intuitive about the emotional state of others. They tend to be relationship focused. At the opposite are people who are task focused. They are practical, organized and traditional. They aren't fond of small talk. Given a choice between socializing and getting a job completed, they prefer to do the job.

If you imagine affiliativeness as a horizontal line, you can see that you shift back and forth depending on the circumstances. Sometimes you feel like "the life of the party" and you are on the far left end of the line — the socializing end. Other times you might have people around you and you think (or even say), "I love you dearly but I wish you would shut-up and leave me alone! I have work to do!" That's when you're on the far right end of the line — the task-oriented end.

Habitually, you favor one of four stages of affiliativeness: very social, mildly social, mildly task oriented and very task oriented. You live in one of the four stages more than the other three.

The Four Success Styles

Combining these two traits, directiveness and affiliativeness, gives us a personality quadrant. Each of the four success styles has its strengths and weaknesses, and no style is superior to any other. All are necessary ingredients to a vibrant, fully functioning workplace.

- Direct + social = orange
- Direct + task = red
- Deferential + task = purple
- Deferential + social = blue

STRENGTHS

assertive

Orange	*Red*
persuasive	decisive
spontaneous	strong-willed
dramatic	high achiever
outgoing	very direct
pursues change	organized
talkative	traditional
adventurous	competitive
dreamer	likes control
opinionated	goal-oriented

Affiliative
social-oriented ··· task-oriented

Blue	*Purple*
loyal	practical
friendly	thorough
caring	factual
loving	reserved
gregarious	persistent
good listener	meticulous
informal	task-focused
agreeable	has high standards
calm	risk avoider

Directive

deferential

Take a look at the Strengths Chart. As you read, you'll see yourself in every corner. As a complex human being juggling vastly different responsibilities, you tap into your talents in each of the success styles. However, through the years you have come to favor one style more than the other three, and that's reflected in your personality. You favor one corner more than the other three.

A strength that's developed to an extreme runs the risk of being interpreted by others as a weakness. The Weaknesses Chart is another tool for determining the corner from which a person habitually operates.

In my workshops, the class participates in an exercise that matches well-known American personalities with the colors. The majority opinion is that President Bill Clinton is Orange, Hillary Clinton is Red, President George Bush is Purple, and President Ronald Reagan is Blue. Besides serving as a fun practice in spotting personality styles, it's a useful way to demonstrate that a person can be any of the four success

WEAKNESSES
assertive

Orange	*Red*
pushy	stubborn
overbearing	dominates
manipulative	closed
disorganized	critical
undisciplined about time	expects immediate results
restless	unapproachable
exaggerates	insensitive

Affiliative ··· *Directive*

Blue	*Purple*
too other-oriented	slow
indecisive	perfectionistic
vulnerable	extra-cautious
impractical	dislikes surprises
dislikes change	withdrawn
	passive

deferential

MOTIVATORS

Orange	*Red*
attention	control
recognition	mastery
achievement	loyalty
excitement	responsibility
adventure	fast pace
spontaneity	

Blue	*Purple*
affirmation	accuracy
kindness	practical
popularity	information
closeness	autonomy
caring	consistency
	perfection

styles and be president of the United States (or close to it).

Each of the four success styles enjoys comfort triggers (motivators) that feed their needs. The oranges are particularly comforted (motivated) by attention paid to them — they enjoy being noticed and appreciated. The reds are comforted by a sense of control over a situation or task. The purples are comforted by a sense of accuracy — they relish the sensation that things are working out as they are supposed to. And the blues are comforted by a sense of closeness — they especially value situations in which care for others (including themselves) is an important element.

There are also discomfort triggers that these serve as de-motivators. A leader who de-motivates someone, even unwittingly, will have a difficult time gaining that person's co-operation in doing what needs to be done. Here are some examples: The oranges feel uncomfortable when kept waiting. Actually, I think most people dislike waiting, but an orange tends to perceive being kept waiting as a sign that he is not special, and he may become defensive or argumentative to draw attention to his needs. The reds are particularly uncomfortable with exaggerated, mushy emotional displays. Lavish praise, for instance, may be interpreted as inappropriate and insincere. The purples have little patience for carelessness and sloppiness. The "YOU CAN DO IT!" just "fake it 'til you make it" attitude of some oranges will be a turn-off. The blues are uncomfortable with insensitive people. A leader who tends to focus on the "bottomline" to the detriment of other people's feelings will lose the confidence and loyalty of a blue.

DE-MOTIVATORS

Orange	*Red*
lack of enthusiasm	time wasters
wanting	irreverence
indecision	laziness
conventional thinking	emotional display

Blue	*Purple*
insensitivity	over-assertiveness
argument	carelessness
insincerity	arrogance
self-centeredness	fakes

Applying Motivators and Avoiding De-Motivators

Is it important for leaders to recognize and respond to different people's emotional needs? Of course it is. What if, for example, you are an orange (motivated by attention) and your employee is a purple (motivated by accuracy) and you're in the habit of dropping bombs like this: "Look, don't put a lot of effort into it, but I need you to give me a rough estimate on the projected sales for the next three years if we merge with the Lopez Company. Also run the numbers on opening either a Mexico City or Santiago office, but without the merger. I need it in an hour so I can make a report at the meeting. I forgot to ask you to do this after last week's meeting. Sorry. Just do the best you can." A purple will likely tense like a deer frozen in the headlights and mutter that you are impossible to work with. She may agree to see what she can do, but even if she gives you numbers by the deadline, don't expect her to feel proud of her work, and do expect resentment toward your loose style.

Here's some sample dialog that could better meet her needs while getting the best job possible: "I forgot to ask you for something I need for the meeting in an hour. Can you prepare a best-guess estimate for three years of projected sales if we merge with Lopez? How about if there's no merger but we open either a Mexico City or Santiago office? How reliable will the data be? What resources do you need now to get this done? When can I have accurate numbers? Thank you."

Here are some other combinations to consider. What if a red continuously barked orders at a blue without regard for the latter's feelings? What if a blue spent an hour gushing to a red about the wonderful opportunities for strengthening relationships that a new project will afford. Consider how an orange would feel in a job with a purple boss who was "all work and no play." The Bible says, "Do unto others as you would have them do unto you." However, different people have different comfort triggers. One style of communicating information is not equally effective among the four success styles. How can you apply knowledge of people's different comfort and discomfort triggers to motivate people to do what you know needs to be done? Here are some suggestions.

Orange

Do:
- Recognize their personal contribution
- Be interactive and animated in your conversation
- Relate your message to his/her ambitions
- Focus on the "big picture"
- Conceptualize necessary actions you want him/her to take
- Let him/her know who else has "bought in"
- Offer "specials"

Don't:
- Dictate
- Get bogged down in details
- Leave things unresolved
- Rely too heavily on written communication
- Talk down
- Be predictable or boring in your approach

Red

Do:
- Be prepared
- Say what you mean — get to the point
- Ask questions, take notes
- Use facts and figures, not feelings, to illustrate
- Refer to objectives, goals, and potential outcomes
- Demonstrate reliability. Keep your word
- Give him/her control by offering options

Don't:
- Chit-chat
- Made decisions for him/her
- Be combative to settle disagreement
- Waste time
- Make excuses
- Make guarantees you can't support

Blue

Do:
- Socialize
- Be open, honest, vulnerable
- Demonstrate trust and need
- Show that you care
- Ask "how" questions to generate discussion
- Show appreciation for contributions
- Choose casual over formal
- Be sensitive to feelings in disagreements

Don't:
- Talk 100% business
- Be afraid to discuss feelings
- Expect immediate decisions
- Threaten or dominate to prompt responses
- Favor facts and figures over people issues
- Patronize

Purple

Do:

- Be analytical in your approach
- Liberally use facts, figures, and substantiation
- Be direct and specific
- Be realistic
- Focus on the task
- Outline action steps
- Provide evidence — and allow him/her to verify your information

Don't:

- Spontaneously discuss important issues
- Try to rush the decision-making process
- Make changes "off the cuff"
- Whine or try to manipulate
- Be disorganized in your presentation
- Interpret "no response" as approval

Putting Knowledge into Action

Take a look at the people you work with the most. Do you see that some individuals have a high need to direct while others are content in a highly deferential role? Do you see that some individuals are highly social in their temperament while others are much more task oriented? Recognizing that different people have different comfort triggers that motivate or de-motivate them will help you meet their needs and bring forth their best behaviors and attitudes. There's no limit to what your leadership can accomplish if other people are motivated to do what you know needs to be done.

ABOUT
DOUG SMART, CSP

*C*all on Doug Smart, CSP, to get participants laughing, learning and leading. Doug works with leaders and teams who want to smooth the bumps of rapid change. He is a successful business owner and a former top salesperson who is authoritative and authentic. A radio personality, keynoter and trainer, Doug has spoken at over 1,000 conventions, conferences, seminars, sales rallies and management retreats.

Doug is the author or co-author of Where There's Change There's Opportunity!, TimeSmart: How Real People Really Get Things Done at Work, TimeSmart: How Real People Really Get Things Done at Home, Reach for the Stars, Sizzling Customer Service, Brothers Together *and* Fundamentals of Outstanding Teams. *In 1998 the National Speakers Association awarded him the prestigious Certified Speaking Professional designation. Contact Doug's office for an information kit on bringing The Get Smart Series to your organization.*

Contact information:
Doug Smart Seminars
P.O. Box 768024
Roswell, GA 30076
℡ (800) 299-3737
℡ (770) 587-9784
fax (770) 587-1050
e-mail: DougSmart.Seminars@att.net

The Leadership Triangle: Purpose, People and Process

by Brian Becker

Have you ever stopped to think about who have been the most influential leaders or mentors in your life? You know— those people without whom, if it weren't for their guidance or encouragement or prodding, you probably wouldn't have amounted to much. Who are the two or three that come to mind immediately? Write their names down right here:

_____

_____

_____

What attributes did these leaders possess that make them so memorable?

_____

_____

_____

I bet you didn't write down "Drives a Lexus, is vice president of marketing at the bank, owns a vacation house in Vail or could retire by age 42." Those things may apply to the people you thought about, but that's not what caused them to have such influence on you.

What you wrote down is much more about who they are on the inside versus what they do, what it says on their business card, or how much money they make. My experience tells me your list probably looks a lot like mine.

- Positive attitude
- Good listener
- High degree of empathy
- Great people skills
- Persistent integrity
- Unconditional acceptance
- Kicked me in the butt when I needed it
- Willing to take risks
- Saw things in me that I hadn't yet realized about myself
- Never stopped encouraging me

Numerous people have had a significant, positive impact on my life, but two people quickly come to mind: One was Raymond Olmstead, my fifth grade band director. I had him as a teacher for only one year, and then he left the field of teaching to be an insurance salesman. I remember well how high his standards were. I sometimes thought they were too high; I was wrong. I also remember he would not accept mediocrity from his students — a quality lacking in many teachers and managers. He expected and demanded we perform with intensity — even in band rehearsals. I particularly remember that he taught us discipline was a key to maximizing high performance, and I remember there were consequences for lack of performance — something lacking, unfortunately, in much of society today.

When I heard Mr. Olmstead was retiring, my initial response was, "Thank goodness! He's so hard on us." My next response was, "How can he leave us? He's so good at what he does, and how will we ever replace him?" Then I cried.

The other inspirational role model was Tim Lautzenheiser, a man I've known for about fifteen years. I'd say he's one of my best friends. In the past fifteen years I've see him maybe twelve times. We've talked face-to-face a total of maybe ten hours — cumulatively. Yet, during these few and far-between short visits, Tim was the one who encouraged me to take risks, to get out of my comfort zone, to use the gifts that God had given me. He was the one who said, "You can do what I do — speak to people and ask them questions — and bring out the best in them and motivate them to be more than they are right now."

For the past fifteen years Tim has traveled 250 days a year and conducts about 200 workshops per year, yet he has taken the time to write me dozens of encouraging letters and still writes to me today. He's been a constant source of sound leadership advice without actually spending much time with me.

So where am I going with this? In the past nine years, my corporate and nonprofit clients and I have dug deep in the area of leadership principles to help them grow professionally. We've discussed issues like qualities of leaders, characteristics of winning employees, developing leadership abilities, and so forth. When I add up all of these qualities, I see two interesting patterns emerge: First, attitude is critical! Almost all of the leadership attributes have much more to do with a person's attitude than with his or her skill or intelligence level. Second, when you categorize these attributes, they fit into one of three categories: *Purpose, People and Process.*

Look at your list of memorable attributes again. You already possess most if not all of these qualities, don't you? You may have been told not to brag, but the bare truth is that you do have them! And if these qualities made your mentors true leaders in your life, then you can have the same impact on people in your life. You don't have to have a Ph.D. or a title or a house in Vail to have a positive and powerful impact on people's lives.

Also, leaders are not born. These traits you admire can be developed to even higher, more effective levels. I began noticing these admirable traits several years ago when researching to find out if my clients' concerns, regardless of the type of organization, were similar. As I pored through my files, my excitement grew; I thought I had discovered some new phenomenon. Indeed, I was seeing these same issues over and over again.

I ran across my old notes from a seminar or class I had taken years ago on Greek philosophy. There it was — not something new, but something very old: ethos, pathos, logos. It was the same as *purpose, people, process* — only stated in different terms.

The Greeks Knew It All Along

Ethos is defined by *Webster's New Dictionary and Thesaurus* as "the distinguishing character, moral nature, or guiding beliefs of a person, group, or institution." It is the source of true motivation — what is on the inside of each person. Some may believe motivation comes from a Zig Ziglar or Les Brown book or tape series, but the truth is if we treat the motivational material like throwing gas on a fire, all we get is a sudden burst of energy that soon burns away. On the other hand, if we treat the material like seeds we plant in a garden in which we are willing to cultivate, water, weed, fertilize, and nurture, then we will get real growth.

Pathos is defined as "a quality that moves one to have empathy or understanding." You see the root of the word in *empathy*. Pathos is about understanding and valuing the differences in people. *Logos* is defined as the systems in place that help things run smoothly, or simply logistics.

Back To My Earlier Research

In reading through my client files, I had simply rediscovered "principles" did exist. What are principles? Webster defines principles as "fundamental truths on which others are founded or from which they spring; a law or doctrine from which others are derived." I say they are timeless truths that should govern the way people operate. I say *should* because much of our society today either does not believe or has not been taught this simple truth. In fact, principles do govern the way life works.

Let me give you an illustration: Let's say that we were on a tour bus, going down the highway. If we were all to look out the same bus window, would we see the same thing? Probably not. Why not? Our own likes, dislikes and experiences draw our focus to different things.

However, would the terrain we see be the same? Yes. In reality, whether we actually perceive the terrain to be the same or not is irrelevant. The sky is really blue, the cactus is actually sharp, the curve in the road is really there, the water in the ditch is really wet. Whether I see or not — whether I want to believe it or not — what *is*, is.

If each of us drew a map of what we saw from the same window, would our maps be the same? No, again based on our perception, likes, and so forth. Similarly, if you were asked to plot your own course using your map, the destination you ultimately reach would be determined by how accurately your map is drawn.

So, is the success of your journey or reaching your desired destination based on your map or on the terrain? It is based on the map — or, more specifically, the accuracy of said map and your ability to read it. What, then, does this have to do with leadership?

The terrain is like timeless principles. (See Illustration A) It *is* reality. Your map is like your values or beliefs, or what you hold dear to you. Thus, the direction you choose is like your ethics or decisions you make. Your destination is then the equivalent to the results you get. So, are the results you get based on the timeless principles? No; rather, they are based on *your* values or beliefs about those timeless principles.

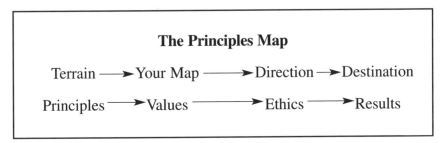

The Principles Map

Terrain ⟶ Your Map ⟶ Direction ⟶ Destination

Principles ⟶ Values ⟶ Ethics ⟶ Results

Let's look at our three main points for this chapter: *purpose, people* and *process*. An organization without a strong sense of purpose will lack direction. A company that does not value its people will lack pride. A nonprofit organization without systems in place to support its membership will be chaotic.

Purpose

Formal purpose or mission statements for organizations were almost unheard of a decade ago. The idea of the personal mission statement is even newer and perhaps more rare. The power that comes from clearly understanding and effectively communicating *where* you want to be in 10-30 years, *why* you want to go there, *whom* you want to serve along the way and *what* is the real purpose of your life cannot be underestimated.

Taking time to reflect on ethos-searching questions helps you clarify your deepest values and beliefs, which are the source of real motivation. It also creates a moral and ethical compass for you. Think of a person who has no strength of purpose, no strong beliefs, no positive direction or goals. This is almost a certain formula for a person with ethical compromise in his or her life.

The Power of Vision

Robert Greenleaf, in his book, *Servant Leadership,* wrote, *"Not much happens without a dream. Behind every great achievement is a dreamer of great dreams. Much more than a dream is required to bring it to reality; but the dream must be there first."*

Developing a vision for the future based on your deepest held beliefs is a powerfully motivating factor. I'm fortunate to know Doris Christopher, president and founder of The Pampered Chef, one of the fastest growing direct-sales organizations in the world. Her dream was to be able to use her skills as a successful home economist to build a company that would allow her to make a sound living and have balance in her life so she could spend time with her husband and two daughters.

Doris started The Pampered Chef in the basement of her home by collecting and selling high-quality kitchen tools that would make homemakers' lives easier and more fun. She held home shows in her neighborhood in the evenings and then packed up the materials the next morning in her basement for delivery. Now in its eighteenth year, The Pampered Chef exceeds $600,000,000 a year in sales and has over

50,000 sales representatives. At the end of one meeting I asked Doris if she ever dreamed that the company would become the tremendous success that it is today. After a ten-second pause a smile slowly crossed her lips. She looked me straight in the eyes and said one simple word: "Yes."

Eighteen years ago Doris had a dream of creating a company that would allow her to live out her deepest held beliefs and values. The company's mission clearly states that they "are committed to providing opportunities for individuals to develop their God-given talents and skills to their fullest potential . . . are dedicated to enhancing the quality of family life by providing quality kitchen products supported by service. . . ." And that's exactly what she's doing. That's the power of focused vision. While there's certainly more to success than that, a compelling vision is hard to stop. Combine that *purpose* with the right *people*, and the proper *process*, and you've got *success*.

Your Vision

Do you think you could benefit from having the clarity of purpose that Doris Christopher had about her future dreams? Here are a few simple exercises to help define your own purpose. Take a few minutes to fill in the blanks and answer the questions below:

Visualize for a few minutes that you're retiring "today," but today is far in the future. Some of your dearest friends are having a party in your honor, and four people are going to talk about the important contributions you've made in your life. One of them is a colleague from work, one a family member, one a lifelong friend, and one from your volunteer life (church, civic group, Little League, or such). If your life has gone exactly like you'd like it to go, in your finest dream of dreams, what would each of these people say about you and the important contributions you've made to each of these four areas?

_____

_____

_____

Based on what those four people said, how would you answer these questions:

What is the true purpose of my life?

_____

_____

Why am I on this earth?

_____

_____

Whom do I really want to serve?

_____

By answering these questions, you will have come to a much better understanding of your own beliefs and values. Now you've got a good start on your personal mission statement. Congratulations! You've just done more soul-searching and serious reflection than most people ever will. The fruits of this process can be dramatic if you use it as a strong foundation for defining the "hats" you wear in life and what you'd like to accomplish (long-term goals) in each of these areas.

Take the time as soon as possible to write down in a journal, calendar or diary, things that will make a significant positive difference in these key areas of your life. Here are some areas to consider:

Physical	Educational
Spiritual	Family
Investment	Philanthropy
Social	Emotional
Business	Financial
Service	Relationships
Vacation	

Defining your purpose and placing it clearly in sight along with a plan of attack and a commitment to action in the above areas will yield positive incremental changes that over time will build a life of fulfillment, challenge and satisfaction — and will allow you to be a true leader to those around you.

People

Do you know the song lyrics, "People — people who need people, are the luckiest people in the world?" I prefer my own version: "People — people who *know* they need people, are the smartest people in the world." Such people realize that no one makes it on his or her own and having diverse skills, backgrounds, experiences and behavioral styles — and knowing how to tap into that diversity — are crucial to a person's success.

Employees in an organization tend to treat each other the way the leaders in that organization treat them. In other words, the organization is a reflection of the leadership's relationship to them. For example, in one particular fast-growing managed care corporation in the midwest, the "people" climate is unhealthy. The company president is fast-paced, brilliant, decisive and confident. However, he is also pushy, arrogant, angry, narrow-minded, and frequently leaves business relationships in shambles. The company has become a reflection of this person's people skills — or some would say, lack thereof. Many employees are afraid to speak their minds for fear of reprisal. The level of trust is low. Camaraderie resembles talking quietly behind closed doors — usually about the boss. If it weren't for a handful of very dedicated and competent managers who constantly work to smooth over hurt feelings, I believe this company would be doomed.

Your organization will take on the personality and style of the people at the top. If you are that person, then what are your strengths? What are your "limitations" (a nice word for "weaknesses")? As it relates to your people skills, where do you excel, and where do you need help? Which of the words in each of the following groups of four describes you best? It will be helpful to visualize yourself in a particular environment (at the office, with family, while selling, etc.).

Circle the appropriate shape after the word in each group.

1. assertive ■	2.systematic ◆	3. energetic ❖	4. analytical ●
1. interactive ❖	2. direct ■	3. thinker ●	4. amiable ◆
1. cautious ●	2. laid-back ◆	3. talkative ❖	4. decisive ■

prefer to:

1. organize ●	2. be in charge ■	3. listen ◆	4. talk ❖
1. structured ●	2. pioneering ■	3. risk-averse ◆	4. catalyst ❖
1. lion ■	2. otter ❖	3. Irish setter ◆	4. beaver ●

Now count and record the number of each shape circled.

❖ = _____   ● = _____   ■ = _____   ◆ = _____

Plot the number of each shape on the appropriate bar of the graph below.

❖	●	■	◆
6	6	6	6
5	5	5	5
4	4	4	4
3	3	3	3
2	2	2	2
1	1	1	1

Realize that although all of the traits you just circled are your strengths, they are descriptive of how you see yourself. And although you are indeed a combination of all of these traits, you can see from this simple graph that the higher the point the more intensity you show for that style. On the other side of that same coin come phrases like these:

❖ Overly emotional
   Too talkative
   Disorganized
   Impulsive
   Daydreamer
   Manipulative

● Critical
   Unsociable
   Worrisome
   Perfectionistic
   Judgmental
   Nosy

■ Impatient
   Forceful
   Attacking
   Stubborn
   Blunt
   Reckless

◆ Resistant to change
   Slow paced
   Indecisive
   Overly accommodating
   Dependent
   Easily manipulated

While these are not generally seen as attractive qualities, they are applicable to all of us, particularly when we are under stress or tired —

or when our resistance is low. Realize that this is only a brief survey, but it still gives a relatively accurate picture of your relationship style. Then, how do you plan to improve your people skills?

_____

_____

What specific steps can you take to improve your effectiveness in building relationships?

_____

_____

Understanding your strengths and knowing how to use them to the fullest, knowing your limitations and being willing to build them up or get help in areas of weakness and flexing your style to build relationships will be key indicators in your long-term ability to lead effectively.

Process

Most people would like success to have an easier pathway, but that's like expecting to harvest a fantastic crop without tilling the soil, planting the seeds, watering and weeding the plants and taking all of the other necessary steps to ensure a healthy crop. Not long ago, I was speaking at a Society for Academic Achievement banquet and noticed a great quote in their program: "The only place where success comes before work is in the dictionary." I can't think of one person I'd truly consider a success who hasn't had to work hard for what they have. That being said, there is more to success than just hard work. A farmer can do all of those things listed above and still not get a healthy product if the conditions aren't right. If it's too hot, too cold, too dry or too wet, none of the plantings will grow. Plus, there's the issue of simply not understanding how to plant crops. I might be a great computer programmer, but that certainly doesn't guarantee my success on the farm, or vice versa.

One of my clients, Page, Inc., of Lamar, Missouri, is one of the leading Midwest companies that focus on rural paging. The owners of Page, Inc., Kent Torbeck and Wanda Dittmer, are excellent examples of visionary leadership. They possess many of the important components needed to lead a fast-growing corporation like long-term vision, passion, integrity, high energy, optimism and focus. However, after several years of outstanding sales, they began to experience growing pains.

While sales and revenues were going up, other things were going down. The processes in place were not equipped to handle increased invoicing, customer service, inventory control and other human resource issues. Fortunately, they were willing to do what some entrepreneurs wouldn't: get help. I introduced them to an expert process consultant from the Kansas City area, Lloyd Arnsmeyer. Lloyd was able to show Kent and Wanda how to improve and streamline many of their human resource and operating processes to help the company work more efficiently.

Streamlining also freed up Kent and Wanda's time to do what they do best: provide leadership, plan, market and sell pagers. Kent told me, "It was painful to admit that we didn't know how to do what needed to be done in some areas. And some of the recommended changes were painful to implement. . . . The biggest problem is that some entrepreneurs will not follow the advice for which they've paid dearly, like changing processes you've invented or firing someone who's been with you a long time, even though they can't do the job."

Ultimately, they were forced to make a choice between trying to do it all themselves or relinquish control of some areas of the business and trusting the advice and talents of others. These decisions are now yielding what I call "short-term pain — long-term gain" benefits for Page, Inc.

Where Do We Go From Here?

Earlier I wrote that this is not just about knowing more, but it's also about making positive behavioral changes. Now you need to create a solid action plan.

Purpose — What is the most important thing you discovered while reading the section about purpose, or your beliefs and values? Perhaps it wasn't what I wrote, but more importantly, what you thought about during that time.

_____

_____

People — Based on the information in this section, what are two or three of your greatest behavioral strengths?

_____

_____

What are two or three limitations?

_____

_____

What are you going to do in response to these limitations?

_____

_____

Process — What process issues are impeding your growth, personally or professionally?

_____

_____

What are you going to do about them?

_____

_____

By when?

I end most of my presentations with a goal-setting session. Once in a while someone will come to me and say, "I'm concerned about setting my goals." I'll ask, "Why?" They usually say something like, "I'm afraid. What if I don' t reach my goals?"

It's not about whether you do or don't reach your goals. It's about progress. It's about using what God-given talent you have to make a difference in this world. If you set average goals and reach them, you can say, "Yee-ha, I'm mediocre!" What good will that do you? The time is now to set your goals to challenge yourself — to stretch yourself. Act on the ideas you've written down in this chapter, and you'll be on the way to being a more effective leader. The lasting effects of this exercise will be both challenging and rewarding for you and those in your life.

ABOUT
BRIAN BECKER

*B*rian *Becker is president and founder of Leaders Edge, LTD., a
*Chicago-based company dedicated to helping organizations grow by
developing leadership and sales skills. Since 1991 Brian has worked with
organizations in Canada, England, Singapore, Trinidad, Puerto Rico and
more than thirty states in the United States.*

*Non-profit organizations and corporations have benefited from
Brian's consulting, workshops and keynote addresses. Contact Leaders
Edge, Ltd. today at (888) 238-4384 for more information about how they
can help you.*

*To find out more about Doris Christopher or The Pampered Chef, go
to www.pamperedchef.com. To find out more about Page, Inc., go to
www.pageinc.net.*

Contact information:
Leaders Edge, LTD.
806 North Fourth Ave.
Maywood, IL 60153
℃ (708) 343-7658
fax (708) 343-9984
e-mail: beckerlead@aol.com

RESOURCES

Brian Becker
Leaders Edge, LTD.
806 North Fourth Ave.
Maywood, IL 60153
✆ (708) 343-7658
fax (708) 343-9984
e-mail: beckerlead@aol.com

Francis Bologna, CPA
Wegmann-Dazet & Co.
111 Veterans Blvd., Suite 1660
Metairie, LA 70005
✆ (504) 837-8844
fax (504) 837-0856
e-mail: FBologna@wegmann-dazet.com

Curt Boudreaux, M.Ed.
The Motivation Man
P.O. Box 422
Golden Meadow, LA 70357
✆ (504) 632-6177
fax (504) 632-4898
e-mail: CurtBoudreaux@cajunnet.com
web: www.nolaspeaks.com/cb

Deborah Dahm
Accredited Seminars & Presentations
3315B Covington Court
Hutchinson, KS 67502
✆ (316) 663-3371
fax (316) 663-3372
e-mail: dldahm@midusa.net
web: www.deblistens.com

Eric de Groot
Exclusively European
P.O. Box 720400
Atlanta, GA 30358-0400
📞 (770) 951-1644
📞 (800) 369-1500
fax (404) 256-5437
e-mail: EadG@att.net
web: www.euroqna.com

Kathy Dempsey
The Learning Agenda
8317 Hamilton Oaks Drive
Chattanooga, TN 37421
📞 (423) 894-8585
e-mail: Kathy@thelearningagenda.com
web: www.thelearningagenda.com

Rene Godefroy
InsightQuest
3589 Mill Creek Trail
Smyrna, GA 30082
📞 (770) 438-1373
fax (770) 438-1373
e-mail: rene@speakingofsuccess.com
web: www.speakingofsuccess.com

D.J. Harrington
Phone Logic, Inc.
2820 Andover Way
Woodstock, GA 30189
📞 (770) 924-4400
fax (770) 516-7797
📞 (800) 552-5252
e-mail: djharrington@mindspring.com

Bob Heavers
Heavers & Associates, Inc.
16278 East Crestline Lane
Aurora, CO 80015
✆ (800) 368-4831
✆ (303) 680-5015
fax (303) 680-5223
e-mail: Heavers@aol.com

Lisa Jimenez
G.C.P. Communications
4691 N. University Drive, Suite 449
Coral Springs, FL 33067
✆ (800) 489-7391
✆ (954) 755-3670
fax (954) 796-0549
e-mail: Lisajmenez@aol.com

Mary Kay Kurzweg
MKK & Co.
215 Stella Street
Metairie, LA 70005
✆ (800) 493-2983
✆ (504) 833-0277
fax (504) 835-7733
e-mail: MKKurzweg@aol.com
web: www.callmarykay.com

Gayle Lantz
WorkMatters
104 Peachtree Road
Birmingham, AL 35213
✆ (205) 879-8494
fax (205) 879-9818
e-mail: Lantz@mindspring.com

Larry Leger
American Management Service
P.O. Box L
Grand Coteau, LA 70541-1011
📞 (800) 992-2920
fax (318) 662-7242

Mike Monahan
M2 Learning Resources
1153 Bergen Parkway, Suite M-181
Evergreen, CO 80439
📞 (800) 759-2881
fax (303) 674-3186
e-mail: M2HRA@aol.com

Gary Montgomery
Prime Time Productions
Louisville, KY 40241
📞 (502) 339-0040
fax (502) 326-4942
e-mail: CoachGary@ICanPlay.com

Connie Payton
5065 Rodrick Trail
Marietta, GA 30066
📞 (770) 516-9418

Rick Segel, CSP
Rick Segel & Associates
One Wheatland Street
Burlington, MA 01803
📞 (781) 272-9995
fax (781) 272-9996
e-mail: rsegel@aol.com
www.ricksegel.com

Jean Houston Shore
Business Resource Group
408 Vivian Way
Woodstock, GA 30188
℅ (770) 924-4436
fax (770) 924-1128
e-mail: Jean@shorecos.com
web: www.shorecos.com

Doug Smart, CSP
Doug Smart Seminars
P.O. Box 768024
Roswell, GA 30076
℅ (800) 299-3737
℅ (770) 587-9784
fax (770) 587-1050
e-mail: DougSmart.Seminars@att.net

Bruce Wilkinson, CSP
Workplace Consultants, Inc.
1799 Stumpf Blvd., Bldg. 3, Suite 6B
Gretna, LA 70056
℅ (504) 368-2994
fax (504) 368-0993
e-mail: SpeakPoint@aol.com

NOTES

NOTES

NOTES